Workbook 1

练习册（上册）

# Zoom In: Intermediate Chinese in 118 Hours

# 118 小时突破中级中文


主　编：LIQUN SU（苏立群）
副主编：WEI-SAN SU（胡未三）
编写者：LIQUN SU（苏立群）
WEI-SAN SU（胡未三）
LU CAI（蔡璐）


MP3
www.sinolingua.com.cn

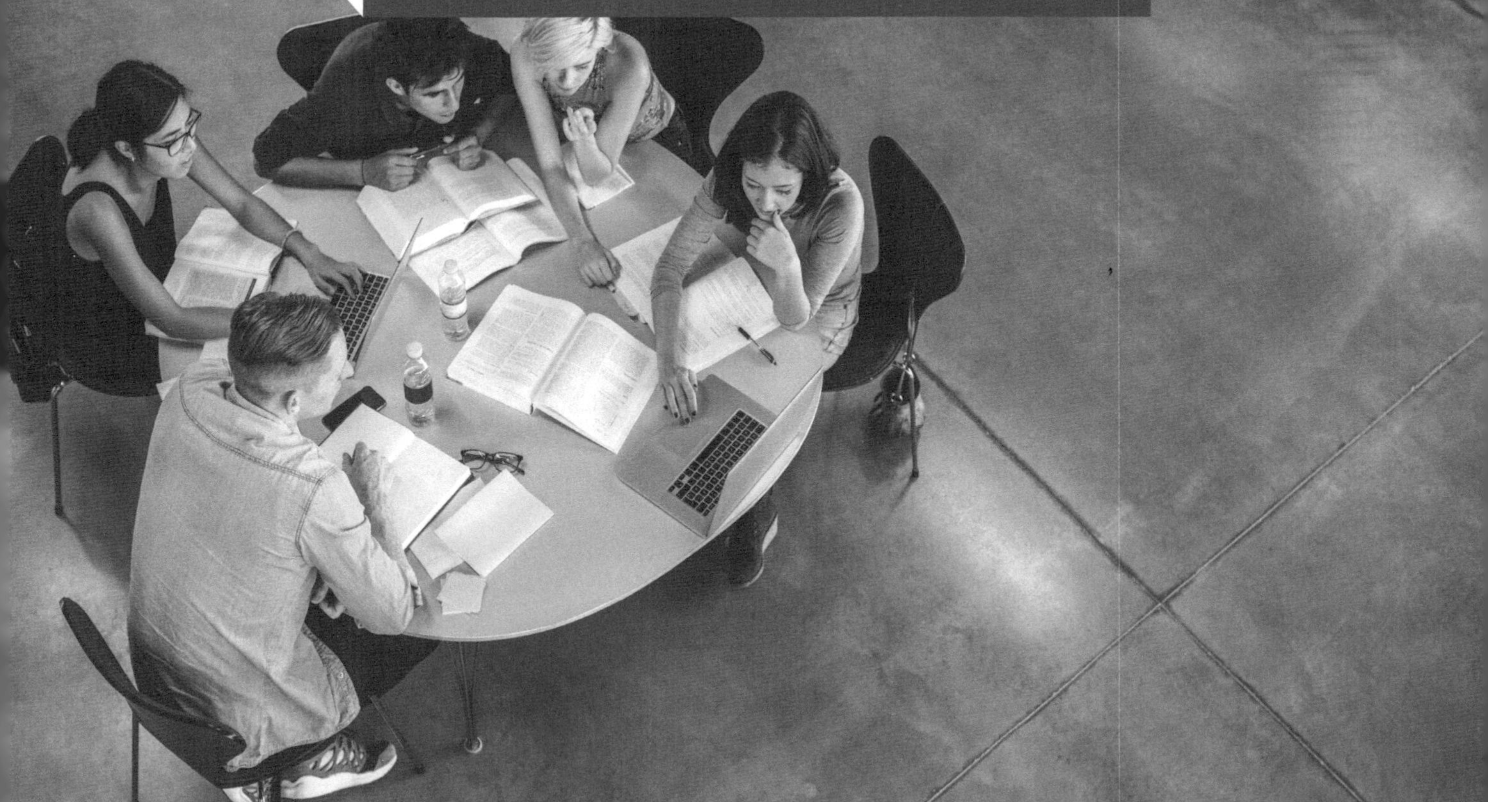


SinolinguA
华语教学出版社

First Edition    2021

ISBN 978-7-5138-2066-0
Copyright 2021 by Sinolingua Co., Ltd
Published by Sinolingua Co., Ltd
24 Baiwanzhuang Street, Beijing 100037, China
Tel: (86) 10-68320585   68997826
Fax: (86) 10-68997826   68326333
http://www.sinolingua.com.cn
E-mail: hyjx@sinolingua.com.cn
Facebook: www.facebook.com/sinolingua
Printed by Beijing Hucais Culture Communication Co., Ltd

*Printed in the People's Republic of China*

# 目录

练习 ································································································································· 1

    Lesson 1 ······················································································································ 1

    Lesson 2 ······················································································································ 4

    Lesson 3 ······················································································································ 7

    Lesson 4 ···················································································································· 10

    Lesson 5 ···················································································································· 13

    Lesson 6 ···················································································································· 16

    Lesson 7 ···················································································································· 19

    Lesson 8 ···················································································································· 22

    Lesson 9 ···················································································································· 25

    Lesson 10 ·················································································································· 28

    Lesson 11 ·················································································································· 31

    Lesson 12 ·················································································································· 34

    Lesson 13 ·················································································································· 37

    Lesson 14 ·················································································································· 40

    Lesson 15 ·················································································································· 43

    Lesson 16 ·················································································································· 46

    Lesson 17 ·················································································································· 49

    Lesson 18 ·················································································································· 52

    Lesson 19 ·················································································································· 55

    Lesson 20 ·················································································································· 58

    Lesson 21 ·················································································································· 61

    Lesson 22 ·················································································································· 64

    Lesson 23 ·················································································································· 67

    Lesson 24 ·················································································································· 70

    Lesson 25 ·················································································································· 73

    Lesson 26 ·················································································································· 76

    Lesson 27 ·················································································································· 79

    Lesson 28 ·················································································································· 82

    Lesson 29 ·················································································································· 85

    Lesson 30 ·················································································································· 88

    Lesson 31 ·················································································································· 91

| Lesson 32 | 94 |
| Lesson 33 | 97 |
| Lesson 34 | 100 |
| Lesson 35 | 103 |
| Lesson 36 | 106 |
| Lesson 37 | 109 |
| Lesson 38 | 112 |
| Lesson 39 | 115 |
| Lesson 40 | 118 |
| Lesson 41 | 121 |
| Lesson 42 | 124 |
| Lesson 43 | 127 |
| Lesson 44 | 130 |

**练习答案** ········· 133

**阅读篇：路在我们的脚下（第三部）（6500字小说）** ········· 153

  路在我们的脚下（第三部）（31—52 单篇注释版）········· 155

  路在我们的脚下（第三部）（31—52 完整版）········· 177

**附录：本册汉字索引表** ········· 186

# Lesson 1  349–360  阿、啊、矮、安、把、般、搬、板、办、半、包、饱

**1. Circle the correct character according to the all-caps word in each catchphrase.**

01) Energy WRAPped by something on the outside is temporarily trapped inside. WRAP is (    ).

    A. 般        B. 包        C. 饱        D. 啊        E. 把

02) When there is a woman in the house, the home will be PEACEful. PEACE/SAFETY is (    ).

    A. 饱        B. 把        C. 办        D. 矮        E. 安

03) It takes a lot of effort to DEAL with things. Sometimes DOing something is like moving a big round stone from one side to the other. DEAL/DO/MANAGE is (    ).

    A. 半        B. 阿        C. 办        D. 板        E. 安

04) This meandering river flowing at the foot of the cliff is the Ah River. The Prefix is (    ).

    A. 阿        B. 把        C. 搬        D. 阿        E. 包

05) This character is split in HALF. Each side is the mirror image of the other. HALF is (    ).

    A. 般        B. 搬        C. 啊        D. 半        E. 饱

06) Someone is holding a tool to fix several wooden BOARDs to the wall. BOARD is (    ).

    A. 阿        B. 板        C. 把        D. 半        E. 矮

07) WOW, the curved river is really beautiful. WOW is (    ).

    A. 板        B. 矮        C. 包        D. 啊        E. 安

08) This surfer is MOVing to a beach with big waves. MOVE is (    ).

    A. 搬        B. 安        C. 般        D. 把        E. 饱

09) This little girl picking grain in the wheat field is even SHORTer than an arrow. SHORT is (    ).

    A. 办        B. 阿        C. 矮        D. 搬        E. 半

10) When you grab a snake with your bare hand, you have to HOLD it close to its head; otherwise, it is dangerous. HOLD is (    ).

    A. 矮        B. 把        C. 包        D. 办        E. 般

11) This man has eaten all the food in the basket and now he is really FULL. FULL is (    ).

    A. 搬        B. 办        C. 啊        D. 把        E. 饱

12) In the water towns of south China, people use the waterways LIKE the public roads. TYPE/LIKE is ( ).

   A. 半   B. 板   C. 般   D. 阿   E. 搬

2. **Match the character with the correct pronunciation.**

   饱   办   搬   把   矮   板   半   啊   包   般   安   阿

   bān   ǎi   ā/ē   bāo   bǎo   bǎ   bǎn   ā/á/ǎ/à   bàn   ān   bān   bàn

3. **Draw the correct tone above each Chinese character OR write a number 0-4 to indicate the tone of each character.**

   0 neutral tone · : without a tone mark, it has no defined pitch and a quick pronunciation
   1st tone - : pitched high and level
   2nd tone / : rising
   3rd tone V : low and dipping to nearly the bottom of the range and then turning up abruptly up at the end
   4th tone / : starting high and loud, then falling sharp and strong to the bottom
   For example: 爱 4 ﹨

   01) 安_____   02) 饱_____   03) 把_____   04) 搬_____
   05) 半_____   06) 包_____   07) 啊_____   08) 般_____
   09) 矮_____   10) 板_____   11) 办_____   12) 阿_____

4. **Listen to the audio recording and choose the Chinese characters you hear.**

   01) _____   02) _____   03) _____   04) _____
   05) _____   06) _____   07) _____   08) _____
   09) _____   10) _____   11) _____   12) _____

   A. 矮   B. 啊   C. 饱   D. 安   E. 搬   F. 阿
   G. 包   H. 半   I. 板   J. 办   K. 把   L. 般

5. **Listen to the audio recording and write what you hear in Chinese characters.**

   01) _____   02) _____   03) _____   04) _____
   05) _____   06) _____   07) _____   08) _____
   09) _____   10) _____   11) _____   12) _____

6. **Listen to the recording and write what you hear in Chinese characters.**

   01) _____   02) _____   03) _____   04) _____

练习 Lesson 1

05) _____  06) _____  07) _____  08) _____
09) _____  10) _____  11) _____  12) _____

7. Translate the following sentences into English. (If there are characters in Chinese sentences that have not been learned, please check them in the "Character List" of the book.)

01) 阿弟，我做的包子很一般，你吃饱了还是只吃了一个半饱？

_____

02) 啊，这个黑板太大了，我搬不动，怎么办？你帮我把它搬走好吗？

_____

03) 我们家电脑的桌子太矮了，你能不能把电脑安在高一点儿的桌子上？谢谢你了！

_____

# Lesson 2  361–372 被、鼻、必、变、冰、才、参、草、层、查、差、尝

1. **Circle the correct character according to the all-caps word in each catchphrase.**

01) The NOSE is very sensitive, and sometimes wearing a mask is useless against air pollution. NOSE is ( ).

    A. 草      B. 参      C. 鼻      D. 被      E. 差

02) Ah, there are two blocks of ICE in the water. The weather is so cold! ICE is ( ).

    A. 才      B. 变      C. 层      D. 查      E. 冰

03) In order to protect this tree, somebody needs to climb up every morning to CHECK if there are any pests. CHECK is ( ).

    A. 查      B. 尝      C. 冰      D. 必      E. 被

04) Throughout civilization, the skins of animals have been cut into pieces to make QUILTs for people. QUILT is ( ).

    A. 才      B. 被      C. 差      D. 层      E. 鼻

05) Wow, there are so many people walking up and down in this five-STOREY building! STOREY/LAYER is ( ).

    A. 参      B. 草      C. 层      D. 查      E. 鼻

06) *The Book of CHANGEs*, or *I-Ching*, reflects the philosophy of CHANGEs of ancient Chinese. CHANGE is ( ).

    A. 冰      B. 参      C. 被      D. 草      E. 变

07) The morning sun illuminates the GRASS. GRASS is ( ).

    A. 草      B. 差      C. 必      D. 参      E. 尝

08) There are only three meat skewers on the barbecue, but so many customers all want a TASTE. How can we have enough? TASTE is ( ).

    A. 尝      B. 必      C. 变      D. 鼻      E. 参

09) A surgery MUST be done, that a needle MUST be inserted in your heart. MUST is ( ).

    A. 才      B. 被      C. 尝      D. 鼻      E. 必

10) I have prepared a music playlist. Would you let me PARTICIPATE in your party, so we can dance to it? PARTICIPATE is ( ).

    A. 变      B. 层      C. 差      D. 参      E. 尝

练习　Lesson 2

11) A person uses a tool to cut some of the BAD crops in the field to feed the sheep. BAD/DIFFERENCE is ( ).

　　A. 冰　　　B. 必　　　C. 才　　　D. 差　　　E. 鼻

12) JUST as soon as the seeds sprout, it will naturally climb up the cross-shaped frame. JUST is ( ).

　　A. 冰　　　B. 变　　　C. 才　　　D. 差　　　E. 被

2. **Match the character with the correct pronunciation.**

　　必　　才　　层　　冰　　参　　鼻　　查　　差　　变　　被　　尝　　草

　　bì　　cháng　　bèi　　cǎo　　céng　　bí　　bīng　　cān　　biàn　　cái　　chá　　chā/chà

3. **Draw the correct tone above each Chinese character OR write a number 0–4 to indicate the tone of each character.**

01) 必_____　　02) 草_____　　03) 层_____　　04) 冰_____

05) 鼻_____　　06) 才_____　　07) 查_____　　08) 差_____

09) 参_____　　10) 变_____　　11) 尝_____　　12) 被_____

4. **Listen to the audio recording and choose the Chinese characters you hear.**

01) _____　　02) _____　　03) _____　　04) _____

05) _____　　06) _____　　07) _____　　08) _____

09) _____　　10) _____　　11) _____　　12) _____

A. 必　　B. 查　　C. 差　　D. 层　　E. 变　　F. 被

G. 冰　　H. 才　　I. 参　　J. 鼻　　K. 尝　　L. 草

5. **Listen to the audio recording and write what you hear in Chinese characters.**

01) _____　　02) _____　　03) _____　　04) _____

05) _____　　06) _____　　07) _____　　08) _____

09) _____　　10) _____　　11) _____　　12) _____

6. **Listen to the recording and write what you hear in Chinese characters.**

01) _____　　02) _____　　03) _____　　04) _____

05) _____　　06) _____　　07) _____　　08) _____

09) _____　　10) _____　　11) _____　　12) _____

7. **Translate the following sentences into English. (If there are characters in Chinese sentences that have not been learned, please check them in the "Character List" of the book.)**

01) 我查过参考书了：这些不是菜，是草，只有草才会长得那么快。再说，要是草，一尝就知道了。你尝尝吧！

_____

02) 虽然今天有会，可是天气这么差，路面上都被包上了一层一层的冰，很不好走，也不好开车，我看你不必来了。

_____

03) 我们一家人的样子都变了：弟弟小的时候，眼睛和鼻子很大，现在不那么大了。

_____

# Lesson 3  373–385 超、衬、成、城、迟、除、楚、船、春、词、聪、答、带

**1. Circle the correct character according to the all-caps word in each catchphrase.**

01) Ancient armies needed weapons and watchtowers to defend their CITY. CITY/WALL is (    ).

   A. 带　　　B. 迟　　　C. 城　　　D. 船　　　E. 超

02) In ancient times, a leather BELT was used to make a bridle for a horse. BELT is (    ).

   A. 聪　　　B. 带　　　C. 衬　　　D. 除　　　E. 迟

03) To manage and express the meanings of language, you use WORDs. WORD/PHRASE is (    ).

   A. 词　　　B. 楚　　　C. 答　　　D. 超　　　E. 春

04) How can I cross the river? The ANSWER is to join bamboo poles together to make a raft. ANSWER/AGREE is (    ).

   A. 聪　　　B. 除　　　C. 成　　　D. 答　　　E. 带

05) In ancient times, knives, daggers and axes BECAME the main weapons in warfare. BECOME is (    ).

   A. 城　　　B. 成　　　C. 春　　　D. 迟　　　E. 聪

06) This athlete is a super charismatic role model. His strict training ensures he always SURPASSes others and wins the gold medal. SURPASS is (    ).

   A. 船　　　B. 楚　　　C. 衬　　　D. 迟　　　E. 超

07) That man fell into the water and was calling for help. A BOAT passed through the rapids to save him. BOAT is (    ).

   A. 带　　　B. 船　　　C. 除　　　D. 聪　　　E. 答

08) No one EXCEPT me can climb up this high wall to get the trophy. EXCEPT is (    ).

   A. 船　　　B. 词　　　C. 春　　　D. 除　　　E. 答

09) In ancient times, there was an INNER LINING inside the coat, and later it developed into a shirt. INNER LINING is (    ).

   A. 迟　　　B. 衬　　　C. 超　　　D. 楚　　　E. 带

10) I am walking the right way, so I can CLEARly see the two big trees in front of me. CLEAR is (    ).

A. 楚　　　B. 衬　　　C. 船　　　D. 春　　　E. 词

11) People who listen with their ears and use their brains must be CLEVER. CLEVER/SMART is (　　).

A. 成　　　B. 答　　　C. 除　　　D. 聪　　　E. 带

12) I don't understand why this parking meter says that I am LATE. I am just a small trolley that walked here. LATE is (　　).

A. 迟　　　B. 词　　　C. 衬　　　D. 船　　　E. 超

13) The sun nourishes the land and life begins to stir. It is SPRING. SPRING is (　　).

A. 衬　　　B. 答　　　C. 衬　　　D. 春　　　E. 超

## 2. Match the character with the correct pronunciation.

城　成　楚　迟　超　带　聪　衬　词　除　答　船　春

chéng　chèn　chí　cí　chuán　chāo　dài　cōng　chú　chéng　chú　dā/dá　chūn

## 3. Draw the correct tone above each Chinese character OR write a number 0-4 to indicate the tone of each character.

01) 楚＿＿＿＿　02) 衬＿＿＿＿　03) 超＿＿＿＿　04) 词＿＿＿＿

05) 带＿＿＿＿　06) 船＿＿＿＿　07) 聪＿＿＿＿　08) 除＿＿＿＿

09) 城＿＿＿＿　10) 成＿＿＿＿　11) 答＿＿＿＿　12) 迟＿＿＿＿

13) 春＿＿＿＿

## 4. Listen to the audio recording and choose the Chinese characters you hear.

01) ＿＿＿＿　02) ＿＿＿＿　03) ＿＿＿＿　04) ＿＿＿＿

05) ＿＿＿＿　06) ＿＿＿＿　07) ＿＿＿＿　08) ＿＿＿＿

09) ＿＿＿＿　10) ＿＿＿＿　11) ＿＿＿＿　12) ＿＿＿＿

13) ＿＿＿＿

A. 词　　B. 带　　C. 春　　D. 答　　E. 船　　F. 除　　G. 成

H. 聪　　I. 迟　　J. 衬　　K. 城　　L. 超　　M. 楚

## 5. Listen to the audio recording and write what you hear in Chinese characters.

01) ＿＿＿＿　02) ＿＿＿＿　03) ＿＿＿＿　04) ＿＿＿＿

05) ＿＿＿＿　06) ＿＿＿＿　07) ＿＿＿＿　08) ＿＿＿＿

09) ＿＿＿＿　10) ＿＿＿＿　11) ＿＿＿＿　12) ＿＿＿＿

练习 Lesson 3

13) _____

6. **Listen to the recording and write what you hear in Chinese characters.**

   01) _____  02) _____  03) _____  04) _____
   05) _____  06) _____  07) _____  08) _____
   09) _____  10) _____  11) _____  12) _____
   13) _____

7. **Translate the following sentences into English. (If there are characters in Chinese sentences that have not been learned, please check them in the "Character List" of the book.)**

   01) 我从家里带来的那件我最喜欢的、春天穿的衬衣，没想到热水一洗就小了。我知道它不可能再变成本来的样子了，除非我再去买一件。

   _____

   02) 当你不懂、不清楚一件事情的时候，不必马上去查词典、看参考书，最聪明的回答，就是"我不懂"。

   _____

   03) "喂，小谢吗？我今天因为工作超时，从城里到上船只有十五分钟了，所以我很清楚，我会迟到半小时。很对不起！"

   _____

# Lesson 4  386–397 单、担、当、灯、地、典、定、冬、短、段、锻、朵

**1. Circle the correct character according to the all-caps word in each catchphrase.**

01) To FORGE a piece of metal and divide it into several sections is hard work. FORGE is (    ).

    A. 锻        B. 典        C. 冬        D. 当        E. 担

02) WHEN you put two chocolate biscuits and a sugar stick on top of this three-layer cake, of course it will be delicious! WHEN/BE/PROPER is (    ).

    A. 典        B. 段        C. 当        D. 冬        E. 单

03) If you want the arrow to hit the centre of the target, it is best done from a SHORT distance. SHORT (distance) is (    ).

    A. 地        B. 当        C. 朵        D. 冬        E. 短

04) This is a SINGLE-speed brand-name bicycle with two mirrors. SINGLE is (    ).

    A. 定        B. 短        C. 单        D. 段        E. 灯

05) It takes a while to cut an object into several SECTIONs. SECTION is (    ).

    A. 单        B. 段        C. 典        D. 定        E. 锻

06) The heavy BURDEN of manual work begins as the sun rises each day, which makes me WORRied. WORRY/BURDEN is (    ).

    A. 当        B. 朵        C. 地        D. 担        E. 灯

07) The STABILITY of a house depends on a correct structure and solid foundation. STABILITY is (    ).

    A. 定        B. 朵        C. 单        D. 段        E. 地

08) This oil LAMP hanging on a T-shaped pole is very strange and beautiful. LAMP/LIGHT is (    ).

    A. 冬        B. 担        C. 当        D. 灯        E. 短

09) During WINTER, children will dress a snowman in a hat and scarf. WINTER is (    ).

    A. 当        B. 冬        C. 典        D. 地        E. 锻

10) Reading all these CLASSIC books can help people learn. CLASSIC is (    ).

    A. 典        B. 定        C. 单        D. 朵        E. 锻

11) A flower bud composed of many petals grows on the twig of a tree. Measure

练习 **Lesson 4**

Word is ( ).

A. 短   B. 地   C. 灯   D. 朵   E. 典

12) LAND is not only the home for humans, but for all the creatures of the world. LAND/SOIL is ( ).

A. 担   B. 冬   C. 灯   D. 地   E. 单

**2. Match the character with the correct pronunciation.**

地   担   典   当   单   定   锻   段   朵   冬   短   灯

duàn   dēng   dōng   duǒ   dān/dàn   diǎn   dìng   dì/de   duàn   duǎn   dān   dāng/dàng

**3. Draw the correct tone above each Chinese character OR write a number 0-4 to indicate the tone of each character.**

01) 灯_____   02) 担_____   03) 定_____   04) 地_____

05) 朵_____   06) 段_____   07) 当_____   08) 典_____

09) 短_____   10) 冬_____   11) 锻_____   12) 单_____

**4. Listen to the audio recording and choose the Chinese characters you hear.**

01) _____   02) _____   03) _____   04) _____

05) _____   06) _____   07) _____   08) _____

09) _____   10) _____   11) _____   12) _____

A. 典   B. 地   C. 担   D. 短   E. 当   F. 朵

G. 段   H. 灯   I. 锻   J. 单   K. 冬   L. 定

**5. Listen to the audio recording and write what you hear in Chinese characters.**

01) _____   02) _____   03) _____   04) _____

05) _____   06) _____   07) _____   08) _____

09) _____   10) _____   11) _____   12) _____

**6. Listen to the recording and write what you hear in Chinese characters.**

01) _____   02) _____   03) _____   04) _____

05) _____   06) _____   07) _____   08) _____

09) _____   10) _____   11) _____   12) _____

7. **Translate the following sentences into English. (If there are characters in Chinese sentences that have not been learned, please check them in the "Character List" of the book.)**

01) A: 你吃过**担担**面吗？听说很好吃。B: **当**然吃过，我每个星期都吃一次，最好的**担担**面是中国成都的。

_____

02) 去年**冬**天我**定**做了一个大**地灯**，**灯**上面有一**朵**红花和两**朵**白云，很漂亮。

_____

03) 这一**段**话不**短**，还有那么多**单**词我不认识，都得查字**典**，所以在**短短**的半小时里，我做不完。

_____

04) 我爸爸每天都**定**时**锻炼**（liàn）身体，就是在最冷的**冬**天，他也**锻**炼。

_____

# Lesson 5  398–409  饿、而、耳、发、法、方、放、风、附、复、该、干

**1. Circle the correct character according to the all-caps word in each catchphrase.**

01) It is fun to make a kite with thin paper and let it float in the sky with the WIND. WIND is (    ).

    A. 放        B. 风        C. 饿        D. 干        E. 附

02) In ancient northern China, some clans regarded the shape of a SQUARE as a spiritual symbol indicating integrity and majesty. SQUARE is (    ).

    A. 该        B. 法        C. 耳        D. 方        E. 发

03) The long-distance runners must REPEAT the same lap around the track dozens of times to reach the red flag. REPEAT is (    ).

    A. 复        B. 放        C. 干        D. 附        E. 方

04) Under ancient law, criminals were PUT by force in the most desolate places to serve their sentences. PUT is (    ).

    A. 放        B. 饿        C. 该        D. 法        E. 风

05) I am HUNGRY! There is food in front of me but I can't reach it. HUNGRY is (    ).

    A. 风        B. 干        C. 发        D. 饿        E. 附

06) This character depicts a person's right EAR. EAR is (    ).

    A. 耳        B. 而        C. 附        D. 风        E. 干

07) An ancient METHOD for creating farmland was to check the field arrangement, wind direction, and drainage systems so as to ensure a good harvest of the crops. METHOD/LAW is (    ).

    A. 发        B. 方        C. 风        D. 该        E. 法

08) The homeowner said to the three: don't argue over every inch of space because we are all AFFILIATEd to each other, like a family. AFFILIATE/ ATTACH is (    ).

    A. 风        B. 方        C. 发        D. 附        E. 复

09) In Peking Opera, this kind of beard indicates not only that this person is elderly, BUT also that he is experienced. BUT is (    ).

    A. 干        B. 而        C. 饿        D. 法        E. 附

10) The tiny alarm clock tells you both that it is a quarter to eleven. You OUGHT TO go to sleep. OUGHT TO/SHOULD is (    ).

    A. 而        B. 附        C. 饿        D. 干        E. 该

11) This is a DRYing rack with two arms, and this is the matter you need to DO. DRY/DO is ( ).

   A. 风    B. 干    C. 而    D. 方    E. 该

12) With a spear, the man can set up and LAUNCH himself forward. LAUNCH/HAIR is ( ).

   A. 该    B. 附    C. 发    D. 风    E. 方

**2. Match the character with the correct pronunciation.**

发    该    耳    饿    法    风    而    复    干    方    附    放

fāng    gān/gàn    è    ěr    fēng    fàng    fù    gāi    fā/fà    fá/fǎ    ér    fù

**3. Draw the correct tone above each Chinese character OR write a number 0-4 to indicate the tone of each character.**

01) 发_____    02) 附_____    03) 耳_____    04) 干_____

05) 法_____    06) 风_____    07) 复_____    08) 而_____

09) 饿_____    10) 方_____    11) 该_____    12) 放_____

**4. Listen to the audio recording and choose the Chinese characters you hear.**

01) _____    02) _____    03) _____    04) _____

05) _____    06) _____    07) _____    08) _____

09) _____    10) _____    11) _____    12) _____

A. 该    B. 附    C. 法    D. 放    E. 发    F. 方

G. 干    H. 而    I. 复    J. 耳    K. 饿    L. 风

**5. Listen to the audio recording and write what you hear in Chinese characters.**

01) _____    02) _____    03) _____    04) _____

05) _____    06) _____    07) _____    08) _____

09) _____    10) _____    11) _____    12) _____

**6. Listen to the recording and write what you hear in Chinese characters.**

01) _____    02) _____    03) _____    04) _____

05) _____    06) _____    07) _____    08) _____

09) _____    10) _____    11) _____    12) _____

7. **Translate the following sentences into English. (If there are characters in Chinese sentences that have not been learned, please check them in the "Character List" of the book.)**

01) 我觉得我的耳朵很干也很热，你看，还有点儿发红呢！我可能病了。你干的事太多了，可能是累病了吧？

02) 来，我告诉你一个很好的在电脑上放上附件的方法。

03) 这些汉字我们都复习很多次了，我很饿，该吃饭了，我们一起去附近的饭馆儿吧。

04) 前天、昨天都没有风。今天我们要出发了，而风起来了，真是运气不好！

# Lesson 6  410–421 感、刚、糕、根、跟、更、故、顾、刮、怪、惯、害

**1. Circle the correct character according to the all-caps word in each catchphrase.**

01) Before you go out it's best to CHANGE in front of the mirror to make you look MORE smart. CHANGE/MORE is (   ).

    A. 故    B. 更    C. 刚    D. 怪    E. 根

02) HARMing others with harsh words is like shooting arrows from three bows at the same time. HARM is (   ).

    A. 刮    B. 糕    C. 跟    D. 惯    E. 害

03) Ancient ruins always contain OLD classic stories that teach modern people what is right and wrong. OLD is (   ).

    A. 害    B. 刚    C. 故    D. 感    E. 顾

04) The left side of the character is a foot, and the character 艮 on the right side means "relevant or corresponding part", so this character refers to a part of a foot: its HEEL. HEEL/WITH/FOLLOW is (   ).

    A. 跟    B. 更    C. 顾    D. 刚    E. 糕

05) The common people speak with one voice: they all FEEL grateful for the soldiers who are protecting their safety. FEELING is (   ).

    A. 害    B. 怪    C. 更    D. 感    E. 根

06) Regardless of how much money one has, it is a good HABIT to use it with good sense. HABIT is (   ).

    A. 怪    B. 惯    C. 刮    D. 刚    E. 故

07) This tempered glass is very strong. Although it has JUST been hit with an axe, it is still intact. JUST is (   ).

    A. 刚    B. 惯    C. 刮    D. 故    E. 顾

08) Above the trunk is the canopy, and below is the ROOT. ROOT is (   ).

    A. 糕    B. 害    C. 跟    D. 更    E. 根

09) This slowly-baked CAKE, made with rice flour and a little lamb fat, is my gift for my mother's birthday. CAKE is (   ).

    A. 糕    B. 感    C. 故    D. 跟    E. 刚

10) Trains can rush out of a tunnel at any time. Birds know this and always LOOK carefully to avoid accidents. LOOK is (   ).

A. 怪     B. 顾     C. 刮     D. 惯     E. 更

11) There is a single eye on top of the pyramid, giving you a STRANGE and sacred feeling. STRANGE is ( ).

A. 糕     B. 更     C. 感     D. 怪     E. 害

12) If a thousand mouths speak at the same time, it will BLOW into a great hurricane. BLOW is ( ).

A. 刚     B. 根     C. 刮     D. 害     E. 顾

**2. Match the character with the correct pronunciation.**

刚    更    糕    感    刮    顾    根    害    故    惯    怪    跟

guài   gēn   gǎn   gāng   gù   guā   gēng/gèng   gāo   gù   hài   gēn   guàn

**3. Draw the correct tone above each Chinese character OR write a number 0-4 to indicate the tone of each character.**

01) 根 _____    02) 更 _____    03) 故 _____    04) 感 _____

05) 刮 _____    06) 顾 _____    07) 刚 _____    08) 害 _____

09) 糕 _____    10) 惯 _____    11) 怪 _____    12) 跟 _____

**4. Listen to the audio recording and choose the Chinese characters you hear.**

01) _____    02) _____    03) _____    04) _____

05) _____    06) _____    07) _____    08) _____

09) _____    10) _____    11) _____    12) _____

A. 糕    B. 感    C. 根    D. 更    E. 顾    F. 刚

G. 跟    H. 故    I. 刮    J. 害    K. 惯    L. 怪

**5. Listen to the audio recording and write what you hear in Chinese characters.**

01) _____    02) _____    03) _____    04) _____

05) _____    06) _____    07) _____    08) _____

09) _____    10) _____    11) _____    12) _____

**6. Listen to the recording and write what you hear in Chinese characters.**

01) _____    02) _____    03) _____    04) _____

05) _____    06) _____    07) _____    08) _____

09) _____    10) _____    11) _____    12) _____

7. **Translate the following sentences into English. (If there are characters in Chinese sentences that have not been learned, please check them in the "Character List" of the book.)**

01) **刚**才宾馆出了意外的事**故**，**害**得**顾**客没有饭吃。

_____

02) 我明天就离开公司：昨天的事，要**怪**就**怪**我们老板。从**根**本上说是他的**感**觉太差，所以我不干了。

_____

03) 面包**跟**蛋**糕**，我**更**习**惯**吃面包。蛋**糕**只有生日的时候才吃。

_____

04) 啊，不好了！我的一百块钱的纸票被风**刮**跑了。

_____

# Lesson 7  422–433 行、河、乎、护、花、化、画、坏、环、换、黄、婚

**1. Circle the correct character according to the all-caps word in each catchphrase.**

01) Ancient Chinese people would build their towns near the gentle bend of a RIVER. RIVER is (    ).

   A. 婚  B. 河  C. 行  D. 化  E. 画

02) If soil is BAD, then the land cannot be cultivated. BAD is (    ).

   A. 坏  B. 乎  C. 黄  D. 换  E. 婚

03) No! This shape is wrong, I want to build a CIRCULar runway, not a runway at the airport! CIRCLE is (    ).

   A. 婚  B. 乎  C. 换  D. 黄  E. 环

04) Banks occupy big BUSINESS buildings along commercial streets where potential customers walk by. BUSINESS/WALK is (    ).

   A. 婚  B. 化  C. 行  D. 画  E. 坏

05) In some parts of North China, women get MARRIED at sunset. MARRIAGE is (    ).

   A. 黄  B. 护  C. 婚  D. 河  E. 环

06) Cleaning your window keeps them looking nice and PROTECTs them from dirt. PROTECT is (    ).

   A. 环  B. 婚  C. 坏  D. 护  E. 黄

07) The fields of the Yellow River Basin are all YELLOW. YELLOW is (    ).

   A. 黄  B. 环  C. 乎  D. 画  E. 花

08) After moving in, I REPLACEd the floor and tiles with my bare hands. REPLACE is (    ).

   A. 婚  B. 河  C. 黄  D. 环  E. 换

09) Zhuangzi, an ancient Chinese philosopher, said that, the CHANGing of life and death is repeated endlessly. CHANGE is (    ).

   A. 化  B. 花  C. 换  D. 画  E. 环

10) The Particle for interrogative or exclamatory sentences is (    ).

   A. 黄  B. 乎  C. 河  D. 护  E. 花

11) I often bring an easel to PAINT landscapes in the fields. PAINTING/DRAWING is (    ).

A. 画    B. 婚    C. 环    D. 行    E. 黄

12) The right balance of chemical compositions in the soil makes the FLOWERs more beautiful. FLOWER is (   ).

A. 黄    B. 换    C. 坏    D. 花    E. 乎

**2. Match the character with the correct pronunciation.**

婚    坏    河    画    黄    环    花    乎    行    护    化    换

hé    huà    hù    huài    huán    háng/xíng    hū    huàn    huà    huā    hūn    huáng

**3. Draw the correct tone above each Chinese character OR write a number 0-4 to indicate the tone of each character.**

01) 乎＿＿＿    02) 换＿＿＿    03) 河＿＿＿    04) 花＿＿＿

05) 黄＿＿＿    06) 环＿＿＿    07) 画＿＿＿    08) 婚＿＿＿

09) 行＿＿＿    10) 护＿＿＿    11) 化＿＿＿    12) 坏＿＿＿

**4. Listen to the audio recording and choose the Chinese characters you hear.**

01) ＿＿＿    02) ＿＿＿    03) ＿＿＿    04) ＿＿＿

05) ＿＿＿    06) ＿＿＿    07) ＿＿＿    08) ＿＿＿

09) ＿＿＿    10) ＿＿＿    11) ＿＿＿    12) ＿＿＿

A. 黄    B. 环    C. 画    D. 婚    E. 乎    F. 花

G. 坏    H. 护    I. 换    J. 行    K. 化    L. 河

**5. Listen to the audio recording and write what you hear in Chinese characters.**

01) ＿＿＿    02) ＿＿＿    03) ＿＿＿    04) ＿＿＿

05) ＿＿＿    06) ＿＿＿    07) ＿＿＿    08) ＿＿＿

09) ＿＿＿    10) ＿＿＿    11) ＿＿＿    12) ＿＿＿

**6. Listen to the recording and write what you hear in Chinese characters.**

01) ＿＿＿    02) ＿＿＿    03) ＿＿＿    04) ＿＿＿

05) ＿＿＿    06) ＿＿＿    07) ＿＿＿    08) ＿＿＿

09) ＿＿＿    10) ＿＿＿    11) ＿＿＿    12) ＿＿＿

**7. Translate the following sentences into English. (If there are characters in**

练习 Lesson 7

**Chinese sentences that have not been learned, please check them in the "Character List" of the book.)**

01) 北京有一条**环**城的**护**城**河**，**河**边有很多漂亮的花。

02) 我妹妹有一个**黄**颜色的手机，那个包手机的皮儿都**坏**了，可是她不在**乎**，觉得能用就**行**，不想**换**新的。

03) 教三年级**化**学课的段老师，刚刚成了家，他是狗年生的，所以他**婚**前跟我说，要我把我**画**好的一只小狗送给他。

# Lesson 8  434–447 或、级、极、急、己、记、季、绩、加、假、检、简、健、讲

**1. Circle the correct character according to the all-caps word in each catchphrase.**

01) The wooden floor I made for my house should be CHECKed carefully. CHECK is (    ).

    A. 讲　　　B. 检　　　C. 己　　　D. 级　　　E. 或

02) The snake on the bamboo tree is EXTREMEly hungry, and must eat the fruit to avoid death. EXTREME is (    ).

    A. 讲　　　B. 加　　　C. 极　　　D. 急　　　E. 或

03) There is a gap between the two bamboo trees on my SIMPLE house. SIMPLE is (    ).

    A. 假　　　B. 检　　　C. 绩　　　D. 己　　　E. 简

04) All silk products need to be checked by hand to be given the GRADE (there are LEVELs A, B and C) before they go to market. GRADE/LEVEL is (    ).

    A. 假　　　B. 检　　　C. 级　　　D. 急　　　E. 简

05) The man needs a HOLIDAY to rest and recharge. HOLIDAY/FALSE is (    ).

    A. 健　　　B. 假　　　C. 加　　　D. 或　　　D. 季

06) Armed with only my axe and my voice, I shall fight and win OR I shall die. OR is (    ).

    A. 讲　　　B. 健　　　C. 简　　　D. 或　　　E. 己

07) In the gym, to increase your strength you must ADD more weight to the machine. ADD is (    ).

    A. 急　　　B. 季　　　C. 检　　　D. 假　　　E. 加

08) One can build good language skills by TAKing NOTE of what one says at all times. TAKE NOTE is (    ).

    A. 记　　　B. 简　　　C. 己　　　D. 极　　　E. 绩

09) The owner of the silk factory has ACHIEVEd great wealth. ACHIEVEMENT is (    ).

    A. 或　　　B. 极　　　C. 季　　　D. 绩　　　E. 健

10) When people are in a HURRY, their hearts will beat faster than normal. HURRY/ANXIOUS is (    ).

    A. 急　　　B. 己　　　C. 记　　　D. 级　　　E. 或

11) The man chose a good spot next to the road to build the structure, so the foundation is very SOUND. SOUND/HEALTHY is ( ).

    A. 极      B. 健      C. 讲      D. 急      D. 假

12) Childhood is a time for growing, just like the growing SEASON of crops. SEASON is ( ).

    A. 己      B. 记      C. 季      D. 级      E. 讲

13) One method of communicating is through SPEECH. SPEECH is ( ).

    A. 简      B 记      C. 检      D. 讲      E. 绩

14) The crawling baby smiled at her SELF in the mirror. SELF is ( ).

    A. 假      B. 记      C. 己      D. 讲      E. 检

**2. Match the character with the correct pronunciation.**

记   讲   加   或   检   健   简   极   季   假   急   绩   级   己

jiǎng   jí   jiàn   jià/jiǎ   huò   jiǎn   jì   jì   jiā   jí   jiǎn   jǐ   jí   jì

**3. Draw the correct tone above each Chinese character OR write a number 0-4 to indicate the tone of each character.**

01) 检_____   02) 假_____   03) 加_____   04) 或_____

05) 记_____   06) 健_____   07) 讲_____   08) 极_____

09) 季_____   10) 简_____   11) 级_____   12) 绩_____

13) 急_____   14) 己_____

**4. Listen to the audio recording and choose the Chinese characters you hear.**

01) _____   02) _____   03) _____   04) _____

05) _____   06) _____   07) _____   08) _____

09) _____   10) _____   11) _____   12) _____

13) _____   14) _____

A. 简   B. 绩   C. 健   D. 级   E. 检   F. 讲   G. 加

H. 或   I. 假   J. 急   K. 记   L. 季   M. 极   N. 极

**5. Listen to the audio recording and write what you hear in Chinese characters.**

01) _____   02) _____   03) _____   04) _____

05) _____   06) _____   07) _____   08) _____

09) _____   10) _____   11) _____   12) _____

13) _____ 14) _____

6. Listen to the recording and write what you hear in Chinese characters..

01) _____ 02) _____ 03) _____ 04) _____
05) _____ 06) _____ 07) _____ 08) _____
09) _____ 10) _____ 11) _____ 12) _____
13) _____ 14) _____

7. Translate the following sentences into English. (If there are characters in Chinese sentences that have not been learned, please check them in the "Character List" of the book.)

01) 明天我不想请**假**,因为会有一个讲**健**身**加**上太**极**的课。
_____

02) 这个**健**身舞**极简**单,真是应该认真学习学习。
_____

03) 这个冬**季**是足球运动出成**绩**的时候,我怎么能不**急**!
_____

04) 请你自**己或**你弟弟把今天**讲**的二**级**的词都**记**下来,明天我要**检**查。
_____

# Lesson 9  448–459 蕉、角、脚、较、接、街、节、结、解、界、借、斤

**1. Circle the correct character according to the all-caps word in each catchphrase.**

01) Traditional marriage customs require that the groom stand at the entrance of the bridal chamber and offer his hand to BRING IN the bride. BRING IN/RECEIVE is (　　).

　　A. 节　　　B. 较　　　C. 接　　　D. 界　　　E. 脚

02) The butcher made three cuts of meat at 500 grams each! 500 GRAMS is (　　).

　　A. 借　　　B. 街　　　C. 脚　　　D. 节　　　E. 斤

03) Roads and STREETs formed around the stores. STREET is (　　).

　　A. 结　　　B. 借　　　C. 较　　　D. 蕉　　　E. 街

04) COMPAREd with normal streets, professional tracks are much better for car race competitions. COMPARISON is (　　).

　　A. 解　　　B. 借　　　C. 角　　　D. 较　　　E. 斤

05) The arrow below indicates the BOUNDARY in between the different plots of farmland. BOUNDARY is (　　).

　　A. 界　　　B. 蕉　　　C. 节　　　D. 接　　　E. 解

06) Let's put up some flowers and hang three red lanterns on the side of the house to celebrate the Spring FESTIVAL. FESTIVAL is (　　).

　　A. 斤　　　B. 节　　　C. 街　　　D. 接　　　E. 解

07) Many people BORROW money from the bank to buy their house, but houses today are worth more now than in past days. BORROW is (　　).

　　A. 脚　　　B. 角　　　C. 节　　　D. 借　　　E. 斤

08) This HORN was cut from the head of a bull. HORN/CORNER/ROLE is (　　).

　　A. 角　　　B. 节　　　C. 结　　　D. 斤　　　E. 蕉

09) When this cow was DISSECTed, the horn was cut off first with a knife. DISSECT is (　　).

　　A. 解　　　B. 较　　　C. 蕉　　　D. 节　　　E. 脚

10) Ten mobile phone users have JOINed together to form this chat group. JOIN/PRODUCE is (　　).

　　A. 节　　　B. 接　　　C. 借　　　D. 结　　　E. 街

11) Is it wise to wear beautiful shoes that are too small and hurt your FOOT? FOOT is (    ).

    A. 脚　　　B. 角　　　C. 蕉　　　D. 较　　　E. 接

12) BANANA trees are dark brown like they'd been burned, and have birds sitting up in the leaves. BANANA is (    ).

    A. 节　　　B. 蕉　　　C. 脚　　　D. 界　　　E. 角

**2. Match the character with the correct pronunciation.**

结　　蕉　　解　　借　　角　　斤　　脚　　接　　街　　节　　较　　界

jiē　　jiāo　　jiě　　jīn　　jiǎo/jué　　jié　　jiē　　jié　　jiè　　jiè　　jiào　　jiǎo

**3. Draw the correct tone above each Chinese character OR write a number 0-4 to indicate the tone of each character.**

01) 角_____　02) 较_____　03) 接_____　04) 斤_____

05) 脚_____　06) 蕉_____　07) 界_____　08) 借_____

09) 街_____　10) 解_____　11) 节_____　12) 结_____

**4. Listen to the audio recording and choose the Chinese characters you hear.**

01) _____　02) _____　03) _____　04) _____

05) _____　06) _____　07) _____　08) _____

09) _____　10) _____　11) _____　12) _____

A. 较　　B. 街　　C. 脚　　D. 蕉　　E. 节　　F. 角

G. 解　　H. 界　　I. 借　　J. 斤　　K. 结　　L. 接

**5. Listen to the audio recording and write what you hear in Chinese characters.**

01) _____　02) _____　03) _____　04) _____

05) _____　06) _____　07) _____　08) _____

09) _____　10) _____　11) _____　12) _____

**6. Listen to the recording and write what you hear in Chinese characters.**

01) _____　02) _____　03) _____　04) _____

05) _____　06) _____　07) _____　08) _____

09) _____　10) _____　11) _____　12) _____

练习 Lesson 9

7. Translate the following sentences into English. (If there are characters in Chinese sentences that have not been learned, please check them in the "Character List" of the book.)

01) 在那个**街角**有**节**日的东西卖，不过我今天没带钱，你**借**我一点儿好吗？

_____

02) 对不起，这车不能**借**你，我妹妹今天**结**婚，我得开车去**接**她，不能**脚**走着去吧？

_____

03) 这个城的东边和西边的分**界**是在这个火车站。

_____

04) 大家听我说，我对这个问题的公正的**解**答是一家一**斤**苹果、半**斤**香（xiāng, prefix of banana）蕉，这样大家就都比**较**高兴了吧？

_____

# Lesson 10  460–471 净、静、境、久、酒、旧、居、句、据、决、卡、康

**1. Circle the correct character according to the all-caps word in each catchphrase.**

01) The competition between plants is QUIET and peaceful. QUIET is (    ).
    A. 静      B. 居      C. 旧      D. 决      E. 句

02) The company has DECIDEd to dredge the water into the two lakes nearby. DECIDE is (    ).
    A. 居      B. 司      C. 决      D. 旧      E. 境

03) The two hands compete for water to get CLEAN. CLEAN is (    ).
    A. 境      B. 句      C. 据      D. 净      E. 久

04) ACCORDING TO the feeling in her hand, the mother can judge if the baby in her womb is healthy. ACCORDING TO is (    ).
    A. 酒      B. 卡      C. 据      D. 决      E. 境

05) The water and ALCOHOL mixture must boil in a special container to be distilled. ALCOHOL is (    ).
    A. 境      B. 决      C. 酒      D. 句      E. 康

06) One must connect words together orally to speak a SENTENCE. SENTENCE is (    ).
    A. 决      B. 旧      C. 居      D. 句      E. 净

07) You need to swipe your CARD to enter the building. CARD/CLIP is (    ).
    A. 卡      B. 久      C. 居      D. 康      E. 句

08) The old man knows that acupuncture takes a LONG time to produce a curative effect. LONG is (    ).
    A. 居      B. 酒      C. 久      D. 据      E. 旧

09) A bird stands on a sign that establishes the BORDER between our land. BORDER is (    ).
    A. 净      B. 据      C. 康      D. 句      E. 境

10) The unborn baby LIVEs inside her mother's body where it used to be empty. LIVE is (    ).
    A. 居      B. 旧      C. 决      D. 康      E. 卡

11) For good HEALTH, you should exercise your arms which will inflate your lungs with air. HEALTH is (    ).

A. 康   B. 静   C. 久   D. 句   E. 据

12) In the digital era, yesterday's technology is OLD today. OLD is (    ).

A. 句   B. 决   C. 净   D. 旧   E. 境

**2. Match the character with the correct pronunciation.**

句   静   卡   据   决   净   酒   久   境   康   旧   居

kāng   jìng   jìng   jū   jù   jìng   jiǔ   jiù   jiǔ   jù   kǎ/qiǎ   jué

**3. Draw the correct tone above each Chinese character OR write a number 0-4 to indicate the tone of each character.**

01) 净_____   02) 康_____   03) 卡_____   04) 久_____
05) 决_____   06) 句_____   07) 酒_____   08) 据_____
09) 境_____   10) 静_____   11) 旧_____   12) 居_____

**4. Listen to the audio recording and choose the Chinese characters you hear.**

01) _____   02) _____   03) _____   04) _____
05) _____   06) _____   07) _____   08) _____
09) _____   10) _____   11) _____   12) _____

A. 决   B. 康   C. 句   D. 旧   E. 久   F. 净
G. 卡   H. 酒   I. 居   J. 境   K. 静   L. 据

**5. Listen to the audio recording and write what you hear in Chinese characters.**

01) _____   02) _____   03) _____   04) _____
05) _____   06) _____   07) _____   08) _____
09) _____   10) _____   11) _____   12) _____

**6. Listen to the recording and write what you hear in Chinese characters.**

01) _____   02) _____   03) _____   04) _____
05) _____   06) _____   07) _____   08) _____
09) _____   10) _____   11) _____   12) _____

**7. Translate the following sentences into English. (If there are characters in Chinese sentences that have not been learned, please check them in the "Character List" of the book.)**

01) **据**说这个边**境**很安**静**，但是不宜**久居**，因为太没有人气了。

_____

02) 我**决**定为了健**康**，再也不喝**酒**了。

_____

03) 你看，这个关**卡**很旧了，不过，这里写着一**句**话："旧虽然是旧，但是干干**净净**。"

_____

# Lesson 11  472–484 渴、刻、空、口、哭、裤、筷、蓝、礼、李、理、力、历

**1. Circle the correct character according to the all-caps word in each catchphrase.**

01) People would kneel before thunder and lighting in an ancient CEREMONY. CEREMONY is (　　).

   A. 礼    B. 裤    C. 口    D. 蓝    E. 力

02) He is using all his strength to hold onto the roots in the cliff. What a dangerous EXPERIENCE! EXPERIENCE is (　　).

   A. 渴    B. 刻    C. 理    D. 历    E. 哭

03) I'm so THIRSTY that I could drink all the water in the pool upstairs! THIRSTY is (　　).

   A. 理    B. 筷    C. 刻    D. 渴    E. 蓝

04) The boy uses a pole to knock down PLUMs from the tree. PLUM is (　　).

   A. 礼    B. 裤    C. 口    D. 历    E. 李

05) This character which means a quarter of an hour exists in many Chinese idioms, so you should ENGRAVE this character into your mind. ENGRAVE is (　　).

   A. 裤    B. 刻    C. 李    D. 空    E. 礼

06) You can eat faster using bamboo CHOPSTICKS. CHOPSTICKS are (　　).

   A. 筷    B. 口    C. 蓝    D. 理    E. 哭

07) There is a good reason why the three streets of neighbourhoods are next to the farmland and water channels. REASON is (　　).

   A. 历    B. 理    C. 空    D. 渴    E. 裤

08) To design an ideal workplace, it is important to leave enough EMPTY space in the building for air to flow. EMPTY/BLANK is (　　).

   A. 空    B. 礼    C. 刻    D. 蓝    E. 理

09) This man came to the warehouse to buy some new TROUSERS. TROUSERS are (　　).

   A. 口    B. 礼    C. 裤    D. 力    E. 哭

10) The process of using certain leaves to make BLUE liquids is carefully monitored by a specialist. BLUE is (　　).

   A. 礼    B. 刻    C. 裤    D. 历    E. 蓝

11) The character for MOUTH is shaped like a mouth. MOUTH is (   ).

    A. 哭      B. 刻      C. 李      D. 历      E. 口

12) The elephant is a symbol of FORCE. FORCE/POWER is (   ).

    A. 力      B. 李      C. 空      D. 裤      E. 刻

13) The character for CRY looks like someone crying. CRY is (   ).

    A. 渴      B. 哭      C. 力      D. 蓝      E. 李

**2. Match the character with the correct pronunciation.**

裤　渴　理　空　历　刻　口　李　礼　力　筷　哭　蓝

kě　lán　kū　kōng/kòng　kuài　lǐ　kè　kǒu　kù　lǐ　lǐ　lì　lì

**3. Draw the correct tone above each Chinese character OR write a number 0-4 to indicate the tone of each character.**

01) 哭_____　02) 渴_____　03) 力_____　04) 蓝_____

05) 历_____　06) 口_____　07) 刻_____　08) 李_____

09) 礼_____　10) 理_____　11) 筷_____　12) 裤_____

13) 空_____

**4. Listen to the audio recording and choose the Chinese characters you hear.**

01) _____　02) _____　03) _____　04) _____

05) _____　06) _____　07) _____　08) _____

09) _____　10) _____　11) _____　12) _____

13) _____

A. 空    B. 裤    C. 渴    D. 刻    E. 口    F. 力    G. 筷

H. 李    I. 理    J. 蓝    K. 礼    L. 历    M. 哭

**5. Listen to the audio recording and write what you hear in Chinese characters.**

01) _____　02) _____　03) _____　04) _____

05) _____　06) _____　07) _____　08) _____

09) _____　10) _____　11) _____　12) _____

13) _____

**6. Listen to the recording and write what you hear in Chinese characters.**

01) _____　02) _____　03) _____　04) _____

05) _____  06) _____  07) _____  08) _____
09) _____  10) _____  11) _____  12) _____
13) _____

7. Translate the following sentences into English. (If there are characters in Chinese sentences that have not been learned, please check them in the "Character List" of the book.)

01) 小李为什么哭了，是不是他们的蓝经理说她的法语口语不好了？

02) 他把他的经历说得很简单，不到一刻钟就说完了。

03) 我累得不得了，口很干，很渴，没有力气走那么远去买那条我喜欢的蓝裤子了。我们还是先去那家"筷子面馆儿"吃点儿东西再走吧。正好里面没有什么人，很空。

04) 我们觉得第一次见我们老师送一点儿礼物比较好，你们说呢？

# Lesson 12  485–496 脸、练、炼、辆、聊、料、邻、留、楼、绿、马、满

1. **Circle the correct character according to the all-caps word in each catchphrase.**

   01) GREEN silk is made by pulling silk through a top wheel and then setting it in the four dye pools below. GREEN is ( ).
   
   A. 练　　B. 聊　　C. 邻　　D. 楼　　E. 绿

   02) Climbing this fire wall repeatedly can REFINE your mind. REFINE is ( ).
   
   A. 炼　　B. 留　　C. 马　　D. 邻　　E. 聊

   03) Two early birds CHATted this morning from five to seven. CHAT is ( ).
   
   A. 满　　B. 料　　C. 聊　　D. 绿　　E. 辆

   04) This looks like a woman holding her hand next to her FACE. FACE is ( ).
   
   A. 练　　B. 邻　　C. 留　　D. 脸　　E. 楼

   05) "Liang" is a Measure Word of vehicles. There are two big trucks in this container. MW for VEHICLES is ( ).
   
   A. 楼　　B. 马　　C. 留　　D. 脸　　E. 辆

   06) This type of STORIED BUILDING is a wood storied structure. STORIED BUILDING is ( ).
   
   A. 绿　　B. 料　　C. 满　　D. 楼　　E. 脸

   07) We have a room, two flowers, and lots of grass, water and love, so we are very SATISFIED. SATISFIED is ( ).
   
   A. 炼　　B. 满　　C. 马　　D. 邻　　E. 脸

   08) NEIGHBOURs are people who live next to you in your town. NEIGHBOUR is ( ).
   
   A. 满　　B. 练　　C. 邻　　D. 辆　　E. 料

   09) The two ponds on the outskirts of the farmland must STAY there to supply water. STAY is ( ).
   
   A. 楼　　B. 邻　　C. 留　　D. 马　　E. 炼

   10) The granary supplies a variety of raw food STUFF to two local shops. STUFF is ( ).
   
   A. 满　　B. 留　　C. 炼　　D. 楼　　E. 料

   11) To make your dance as smooth as silk requires repeated PRACTICE. PRACTICE is ( ).
   
   A. 练　　B. 聊　　C. 炼　　D. 楼　　E. 绿

练习   Lesson 12

12) This character looks like a HORSE head and a powerful big hoof! HORSE is (    ).
   A. 料    B. 绿    C. 脸    D. 马    E. 辆

2. Match the character with the correct pronunciation.

   炼   练   楼   脸   邻   料   马   聊   满   绿   留   辆

   liú   lǜ   lín   liǎn   mǎn   liáo   liàng   lóu   liàn   mǎ   liàn   liào

3. Draw the correct tone above each Chinese character OR write a number 0-4 to indicate the tone of each character.

   01) 马_____   02) 邻_____   03) 楼_____   04) 脸_____
   05) 练_____   06) 料_____   07) 炼_____   08) 绿_____
   09) 满_____   10) 聊_____   11) 留_____   12) 辆_____

4. Listen to the audio recording and choose the Chinese characters you hear.

   01) _____   02) _____   03) _____   04) _____
   05) _____   06) _____   07) _____   08) _____
   09) _____   10) _____   11) _____   12) _____

   A. 脸    B. 留    C. 邻    D. 练    E. 聊    F. 料
   G. 辆    H. 炼    I. 楼    J. 绿    K. 马    L. 满

5. Listen to the audio recording and write what you hear in Chinese characters.

   01) _____   02) _____   03) _____   04) _____
   05) _____   06) _____   07) _____   08) _____
   09) _____   10) _____   11) _____   12) _____

6. Listen to the recording and write what you hear in Chinese characters.

   01) _____   02) _____   03) _____   04) _____
   05) _____   06) _____   07) _____   08) _____
   09) _____   10) _____   11) _____   12) _____

7. Translate the following sentences into English. (If there are characters in Chinese sentences that have not been learned, please check them in the "Character List" of the book.)

   01) 李太太和她（的）楼上的邻居天天见面聊天，不聊满一个小时还不满足。

02) 锻**炼**身体和上学做课后的**练**习一样，不要**留**到第二天去做，当天的事，当天**马**上做完。

___

03) 谁都没有**料**到李医生昨天买了一**辆绿**色的车，有人问他为什么的时候，他的**脸**一下子就红了，**马**上笑着说，这是他太太最喜欢的颜色。

___

# Lesson 13  497–508 冒、帽、末、目、拿、南、难、鸟、努、爬、怕、盘

### 1. Circle the correct character according to the all-caps word in each catchphrase.

01) The PLATE is already set with fish, rice and chopsticks. PLATE is ( ).
   A. 盘　　B. 努　　C. 怕　　D. 末　　E. 帽

02) I am AFRAID that this toxic smell came from that broken white bottle! AFRAID/FEAR is ( ).
   A. 爬　　B. 目　　C. 拿　　D. 怕　　E. 难

03) The water EVAPORATEs through several layers. EVAPORATE is ( ).
   A. 盘　　B. 冒　　C. 帽　　D. 爬　　E. 末

04) Using a trap to catch a bird with a long tail is very DIFFICULT. DIFFICULT/DISASTER is ( ).
   A. 帽　　B. 难　　C. 目　　D. 努　　E. 鸟

05) The determined snake slowly CLIMBs up the mountain. CLIMB is ( ).
   A. 帽　　B. 鸟　　C. 爬　　D. 难　　E. 冒

06) Put your hands together and PICK UP your favorite things. PICK UP is ( ).
   A. 拿　　B. 怕　　C. 末　　D. 难　　E. 帽

07) This cloth CAP can keep both your head and ears very warm. CAP is ( ).
   A. 拿　　B. 帽　　C. 目　　D. 怕　　E. 盘

08) In the northern hemisphere, trees growing on the SOUTH of the mountain get more sunshine. SOUTH is ( ).
   A. 南　　B. 努　　C. 末　　D. 鸟　　E. 难

09) This BIRD has a hooked mouth and big wing. BIRD is ( ).
   A. 鸟　　B. 拿　　C. 爬　　D. 努　　E. 帽

10) Don't climb out to the END of the long tree branch or you will fall! END is ( ).
   A. 末　　B. 目　　C. 鸟　　D. 怕　　E. 盘

11) Slaves would use all their strength to do HARD WORK all day. HARD WORK is ( ).
   A. 目　　B. 难　　C. 努　　D. 爬　　E. 盘

12) The EYE is also called "Mu", which is composed of the eye socket, the eyeball, and the pupil. EYE is ( ).
   A. 爬　　B. 末　　C. 努　　D. 目　　D. 怕

2. **Match the character with the correct pronunciation.**

帽　爬　盘　努　冒　拿　目　难　怕　末　南　鸟

mào　ná　mù　pá　mò　nǔ　mào　niǎo　pán　pà　nán　nán/nàn

3. **Draw the correct tone above each Chinese character OR write a number 0-4 to indicate the tone of each character.**

01) 拿_____　02) 爬_____　03) 怕_____　04) 努_____
05) 南_____　06) 帽_____　07) 目_____　08) 难_____
09) 盘_____　10) 末_____　11) 冒_____　12) 鸟_____

4. **Listen to the audio recording and choose the Chinese characters you hear.**

01) _____　02) _____　03) _____　04) _____
05) _____　06) _____　07) _____　08) _____
09) _____　10) _____　11) _____　12) _____

A. 鸟　　B. 怕　　C. 难　　D. 冒　　E. 末　　F. 努
G. 目　　H. 盘　　I. 南　　J. 帽　　K. 爬　　L. 拿

5. **Listen to the audio recording and write what you hear in Chinese characters.**

01) _____　02) _____　03) _____　04) _____
05) _____　06) _____　07) _____　08) _____
09) _____　10) _____　11) _____　12) _____

6. **Listen to the recording and write what you hear in Chinese characters.**

01) _____　02) _____　03) _____　04) _____
05) _____　06) _____　07) _____　08) _____
09) _____　10) _____　11) _____　12) _____

7. **Translate the following sentences into English. (If there are characters in Chinese sentences that have not been learned, please check them in the "Character List" of the book.)**

01) 我可能感**冒**了，很**怕**冷，今天刮**南**风，出去不**拿**着**帽**子不行。

_____

02) 大家都应该要有爱干净的好习惯，吃完了饭要把筷子和**盘**子洗干净。

_____

03) 经理告诉我，他说，现在做的这个电视节**目**叫"**鸟**的末日"。这个节目很**难**做，不过这些人很**努**力，为了不被**鸟**看见，担心**鸟**见到他们就会害**怕**，所以他们都穿着绿色的衣服，**爬**到很高的树上。

# Lesson 14  509–520 胖、皮、啤、片、平、瓶、其、奇、骑、且、轻、清

**1. Circle the correct character according to the all-caps word in each catchphrase.**

01) This basket with legs is very useful. IT can be packed with many things. IT/THAT is (    ).

   A. 清     B. 轻     C. 奇     D. 其     E. 平

02) It's very STRANGE to see this adult walking with a pole on this sharp object. STRANGE is (    ).

   A. 皮     B. 片     C. 其     D. 胖     E. 奇

03) You're getting FAT! Your body is a half width larger than last year! FAT is (    ).

   A. 胖     B. 清     C. 且     D. 骑     E. 瓶

04) This tall earthenware BOTTLE with a handle is handmade. BOTTLE is (    ).

   A. 清     B. 啤     C. 皮     D. 瓶     E. 奇

05) Trees can grow healthy and tall with clean, CLEAR water. CLEAR is (    ).

   A. 片     B. 骑     C. 清     D. 皮     E. 轻

06) BEER feels very undervalued: why is its price so much lower than other alcohol? BEER is (    ).

   A. 啤     B. 清     C. 其     D. 轻     E. 且

07) The character for ADD looks like a three-step ladder; the sentence is not finished until more words are ADDed. ADD/EVEN MORE is (    ).

   A. 且     B. 骑     C. 胖     D. 奇     E. 轻

08) The man RIDEs the horse very strangely. RIDE is (    ).

   A. 清     B. 骑     C. 且     D. 平     E. 啤

09) The SKIN of animals like cows is taken off to make clothing and shoes. SKIN is (    ).

   A. 清     B. 胖     C. 皮     D. 片     E. 啤

10) This structure is very balanced because the horizon line is FLAT. FLAT/LEVEL is (    ).

   A. 片     B. 平     C. 瓶     D. 且     E. 轻

11) Cutting wood into PIECEs requires a special wood saw. PIECE is (    ).

   A. 骑     B. 皮     C. 啤     D. 清     E. 片

12) To get up the mountain road, our vehicle should be LIGHT. LIGHT is ( ).

    A. 胖　　　B. 奇　　　C. 轻　　　D. 且　　　E. 清

**2. Match the character with the correct pronunciation.**

片　　胖　　清　　奇　　骑　　瓶　　平　　啤　　皮　　其　　且　　轻

pí　qīng　píng　pàng　qí　qiě　pí　qí　píng　qí　qīng　piàn/piān

**3. Draw the correct tone above each Chinese character OR write a number 0-4 to indicate the tone of each character.**

01) 胖_____　02) 其_____　03) 奇_____　04) 啤_____

05) 清_____　06) 平_____　07) 轻_____　08) 且_____

09) 骑_____　10) 皮_____　11) 片_____　12) 瓶_____

**4. Listen to the audio recording and choose the Chinese characters you hear.**

01) _____　02) _____　03) _____　04) _____

05) _____　06) _____　07) _____　08) _____

09) _____　10) _____　11) _____　12) _____

A. 胖　　B. 奇　　C. 皮　　D. 啤　　E. 片　　F. 清

G. 瓶　　H. 平　　I. 骑　　J. 其　　K. 且　　L. 轻

**5. Listen to the audio recording and write what you hear in Chinese characters.**

01) _____　02) _____　03) _____　04) _____

05) _____　06) _____　07) _____　08) _____

09) _____　10) _____　11) _____　12) _____

**6. Listen to the recording and write what you hear in Chinese characters.**

01) _____　02) _____　03) _____　04) _____

05) _____　06) _____　07) _____　08) _____

09) _____　10) _____　11) _____　12) _____

**7. Translate the following sentences into English. (If there are characters in Chinese sentences that have not been learned, please check them in the "Character List" of the book.)**

01) 你平时啤酒喝多了，而且一天喝三瓶，所以胖了。

02) 你看这位**骑**马的先生，样子很**平**常，可是穿的大衣很**奇**怪，颜色看不**清**，好像一半是咖啡色，一半是米黄色，真的很难看。

03) 这一**片**地方我都看过了，除了这个**皮**包店，**其**他的店都没有。就买这个吧，这个**皮**包颜色不错，而**且**很**轻**，再说也不贵。

# Lesson 15  521–532  秋、求、趣、裙、容、如、赛、伞、扫、山、衫、烧

**1. Circle the correct character according to the all-caps word in each catchphrase.**

01) This character looks just like an UMBRELLA. UMBRELLA is (    ).

   A. 伞      B. 扫      C. 趣      D. 裙      E. 秋

02) In a rugby MATCH, players compete head-to-head to get the ball which is under them. MATCH is (    ).

   A. 趣      B. 赛      C. 裙      D. 秋      E. 伞

03) Even witches must hold on to their BROOMs when whizzing through the air! BROOM/SWEEP is (    ).

   A. 如      B. 扫      C. 衫      D. 趣      E. 山

04) AUTUMN is the best time to roast corn on the fire! AUTUMN is (    ).

   A. 求      B. 烧      C. 秋      D. 扫      E. 山

05) Women have no trouble speaking from the heart. Their words and feelings are often very SIMILAR. SIMILAR is (    ).

   A. 如      B. 趣      C. 赛      D. 扫      E. 容

06) The fire BURNs next to the pile of toppling bricks. BURN is (    ).

   A. 容      B. 求      C. 烧      D. 衫      E. 扫

07) I had to ASK FOR an animal hide to keep me warm last night. ASK FOR is (    ).

   A. 裙      B. 伞      C. 求      D. 秋      E. 如

08) Even though the valley is huge and deep, the roof of the heaven can still ACCOMMODATE it. ACCOMMODATE is (    ).

   A. 山      B. 烧      C. 裙      D. 趣      E. 容

09) This looks like a SHIRT drying in the sunlight. SHIRT is (    ).

   A. 赛      B. 裙      C. 趣      D. 如      E. 衫

10) Although it is FUN to listen to music while walking, it can be dangerous if you don't pay attention! FUN/INTERESTING is (    ).

   A. 趣      B. 衫      C. 扫      D. 容      E. 求

11) This character looks just like a MOUNTAIN. MOUNTAIN is (    ).

   A. 秋      B. 如      C. 裙      D. 山      E. 衫

12) Before buying a SKIRT, you should feel the fabric and notice if it has been recommended by word of mouth. SKIRT is (    ).

A. 裙　　　B. 烧　　　C. 秋　　　D. 趣　　　E. 赛

**2. Match the character with the correct pronunciation.**

趣　　求　　扫　　秋　　容　　山　　赛　　烧　　裙　　如　　衫　　伞

qún　qù　shān　qiú　shāo　sǎo　rú　qiū　sǎn　shān　róng　sài

**3. Draw the correct tone above each Chinese character OR write a number 0-4 to indicate the tone of each character.**

01) 山_____　02) 秋_____　03) 如_____　04) 裙_____
05) 伞_____　06) 赛_____　07) 趣_____　08) 烧_____
09) 求_____　10) 容_____　11) 衫_____　12) 扫_____

**4. Listen to the audio recording and choose the Chinese characters you hear.**

01) _____　02) _____　03) _____　04) _____
05) _____　06) _____　07) _____　08) _____
09) _____　10) _____　11) _____　12) _____

A. 扫　　B. 秋　　C. 伞　　D. 求　　E. 容　　F. 赛
G. 裙　　H. 烧　　I. 趣　　J. 衫　　K. 山　　L. 如

**5. Listen to the audio recording and write what you hear in Chinese characters.**

01) _____　02) _____　03) _____　04) _____
05) _____　06) _____　07) _____　08) _____
09) _____　10) _____　11) _____　12) _____

**6. Listen to the recording and write what you hear in Chinese characters.**

01) _____　02) _____　03) _____　04) _____
05) _____　06) _____　07) _____　08) _____
09) _____　10) _____　11) _____　12) _____

**7. Translate the following sentences into English. (If there are characters in Chinese sentences that have not been learned, please check them in the "Character List" of the book.)**

01) 秋天来了，姐姐求我从法国给她买一条裙子和一件衬衫。

02) 我喜欢跳**伞**和**赛**车两个运动，因为很有**趣**。

03) 听说山鸡红**烧**的很好吃，可是现在买不到山鸡，所以今天我只好买平常的鸡**烧**给客人吃了。

04) **如**果你有时间，有兴**趣**跟我一起去**扫**雪吗？

05) 雪很大，路面**容**易打滑，得在下班以前把路上的雪清**扫**干净。

# Lesson 16  533–544 声、实、史、世、市、瘦、叔、舒、束、树、数、刷

### 1. Circle the correct character according to the all-caps word in each catchphrase.

01) To worry about getting the roof over your head is a very PRACTICAL concern. PRACTICAL is ( ).

   A. 实　　　B. 束　　　C. 史　　　D. 世　　　E. 数

02) In a clothing store, a dress with a BUNCHed waist will attract many women. BUNCH is ( ).

   A. 刷　　　B. 舒　　　C. 市　　　D. 束　　　E. 史

03) These TREE seedlings were planted too close. TREE is ( ).

   A. 世　　　B. 舒　　　C. 叔　　　D. 刷　　　E. 树

04) A SOUND should be made when a car speeds by, and cameras can record the violation. SOUND is ( ).

   A. 声　　　B. 树　　　C. 瘦　　　D. 市　　　E. 刷

05) We found a COMFORTABLE hotel by searching online. COMFORTABLE is ( ).

   A. 树　　　B. 市　　　C. 史　　　D. 舒　　　E. 声

06) Three generations more or less make a CENTURY. CENTURY is ( ).

   A. 实　　　B. 世　　　C. 史　　　D. 束　　　E. 数

07) Our female math teacher's mental arithmetic is so good that she gets the correct NUMBER faster than a calculator! NUMBER/TO COUNT is ( ).

   A. 世　　　B. 数　　　C. 束　　　D. 史　　　E. 实

08) Ink and a brush is necessary when writing down facts in the HISTORY books. HISTORY is ( ).

   A. 舒　　　B. 刷　　　C. 史　　　D. 瘦　　　E. 声

09) This machine has a SCRUB and a rag, and is very effective for wiping windows. SCRUB is ( ).

   A. 实　　　B. 世　　　C. 刷　　　D. 叔　　　E. 束

10) This THIN man looks sick wearing a straw hat and supported with a crutch. THIN is ( ).

   A. 舒　　　B. 瘦　　　C. 数　　　D. 史　　　E. 声

11) UNCLEs are in between the younger and older generations. UNCLE is ( ).

   A. 世　　　B. 实　　　C. 瘦　　　D. 数　　　E. 叔

12) Stock MARKET values are seen on the screens of many computers; they go up and down every day and are extremely difficult to predict. MARKET is ( ).

A. 声　　　B. 市　　　C. 史　　　D. 刷　　　E. 束

**2. Match the character with the correct pronunciation.**

实　舒　刷　瘦　叔　声　束　市　史　数　树　世

shí　shǔ/shù　shì　shū　shù　shēng　shǐ　shū　shù　shuā　shì　shòu

**3. Draw the correct tone above each Chinese character OR write a number 0-4 to indicate the tone of each character.**

01) 声_____　　02) 束_____　　03) 数_____　　04) 刷_____

05) 树_____　　06) 实_____　　07) 舒_____　　08) 叔_____

09) 史_____　　10) 市_____　　11) 世_____　　12) 瘦_____

**4. Listen to the audio recording and choose the Chinese characters you hear.**

01) _____　　02) _____　　03) _____　　04) _____

05) _____　　06) _____　　07) _____　　08) _____

09) _____　　10) _____　　11) _____　　12) _____

A. 世　　B. 舒　　C. 声　　D. 束　　E. 瘦　　F. 数

G. 市　　H. 刷　　I. 树　　J. 实　　K. 史　　L. 叔

**5. Listen to the audio recording and write what you hear in Chinese characters.**

01) _____　　02) _____　　03) _____　　04) _____

05) _____　　06) _____　　07) _____　　08) _____

09) _____　　10) _____　　11) _____　　12) _____

**6. Listen to the recording and write what you hear in Chinese characters.**

01) _____　　02) _____　　03) _____　　04) _____

05) _____　　06) _____　　07) _____　　08) _____

09) _____　　10) _____　　11) _____　　12) _____

**7. Translate the following sentences into English. (If there are characters in Chinese sentences that have not been learned, please check them in the "Character List" of the book.)**

01) 我在大学学的是**世界历史**，你呢？

_____

02) 我昨天把我**叔叔**上个月买的房子**刷**了。这个房子的后面有不少大苹果**树**，所以我就买了十几**束**花放在房子的里面，这样里里外外看起来很漂亮也很**舒**服。我**叔叔**搬进来的时候，一定会喜欢。

_____

03) 我们班有很**瘦**的学生，平时不出**声**，也不怎么努力，可是**实**在是个天才，每次的全**市数**学比赛，他都**数**一**数**二。

_____

# Lesson 17  545–556 双、算、特、疼、梯、提、甜、调、铁、头、突、图

**1. Circle the correct character according to the all-caps word in each catchphrase.**

01) This looks like a PICTURE of a bird in a winter city. PICTURE is (    ).

    A. 头        B. 图        03 双        04 算        05 突

02) Use your hand to CARRY or LIFT something on the right path under the sun. CARRY/LIFT is (    ).

    A. 铁        B. 算        C. 提        D. 图        E. 梯

03) This character looks like a LADDER going up a tree. LADDER/STAIRS is (    ).

    A. 梯        B. 调        C. 疼        D. 甜        E. 铁

04) A dog rushed out of a cave and scared me SUDDENly. SUDDEN is (    ).

    A. 特        B. 双        C. 梯        D. 突        E. 甜

05) When the tongue tastes sweet water, the result is SWEET. SWEET is (    ).

    A. 头        B. 调        C. 甜        D. 疼        E. 铁

06) The HEAD is where a person's brain is located, and is the centre of thought and emotion. HEAD is (    ).

    A. 头        B. 梯        C. 提        D. 算        E. 特

07) Inflammations in the body can always cause PAIN. PAIN is (    ).

    A. 提        B. 疼        C. 铁        D. 甜        E. 突

08) To move people with spoken language, you need to ADJUST the sound quality and volume of your voice in a comprehensive way. ADJUST/ALLOCATE is (    ).

    A. 特        B. 图        C. 算        D. 突        E. 调

09) The radical for this word is metal, and the right side means lost value. Combined, it means a low-priced metal which is IRON. IRON is (    ).

    A. 双        B. 铁        C. 梯        D. 甜        E. 算

10) The word on the left is a cow and on the right is a temple. In ancient times, people believed cows had a SPECIAL significance. SPECIAL is (    ).

    A. 特        B. 突        C. 双        D. 头        E. 提

11) You need your hands and eyes to CALCULATE on an abacus. CALCULATE is (    ).

    A. 疼        B. 算        C. 甜        D. 图        E. 铁

12) One chopstick plus one chopstick makes A PAIR. A PAIR is (    ).

    A. 疼      B. 双      C. 突      D. 梯      E. 调

2. Match the character with the correct pronunciation.

调　　算　　双　　提　　图　　头　　疼　　铁　　梯　　特　　甜　　突

tè　　tū　　tóu　　diào/tiáo　　tú　　shuāng　　tiě　　tī　　tián　　tí　　suàn　　téng

3. Draw the correct tone above each Chinese character OR write a number 0-4 to indicate the tone of each character.

01) 疼_____    02) 提_____    03) 算_____    04) 双_____

05) 铁_____    06) 突_____    07) 梯_____    08) 调_____

09) 图_____    10) 特_____    11) 甜_____    12) 头_____

4. Listen to the audio recording and choose the Chinese characters you hear.

01) _____    02) _____    03) _____    04) _____

05) _____    06) _____    07) _____    08) _____

09) _____    10) _____    11) _____    12) _____

A. 疼    B. 提    C. 算    D. 图    E. 甜    F. 双

G. 头    H. 调    I. 特    J. 梯    K. 突    L. 铁

5. Listen to the audio recording and write what you hear in Chinese characters.

01) _____    02) _____    03) _____    04) _____

05) _____    06) _____    07) _____    08) _____

09) _____    10) _____    11) _____    12) _____

6. Listen to the recording and write what you hear in Chinese characters.

01) _____    02) _____    03) _____    04) _____

05) _____    06) _____    07) _____    08) _____

09) _____    10) _____    11) _____    12) _____

7. Translate the following sentences into English. (If there are characters in Chinese sentences that have not been learned, please check them in the "Character List" of the book.)

01) 空调坏了，我们有梯子吗？

_____

02) 今天**特**别冷，我**突**然感冒了，**头**很**疼**；没想到，我**双**生的弟弟也感冒了。
___

03) 你的手**提**电脑上有没有北京的地**铁图**？
___

04) 我**算**了一下，**甜**点心比不**甜**的点心便宜得多。
___

# Lesson 18  557–568 腿、碗、万、网、忘、位、文、闻、物、戏、夏、鲜

### 1. Circle the correct character according to the all-caps word in each catchphrase.

01) People should show respect to those who have achieved their POSITION through ability and hard work. POSITION is (    ).

    A. 位　　　B. 鲜　　　C. 闻　　　D. 忘　　　E. 物

02) A plate of FRESH fish and lamb kebabs is really a delicious meal! FRESH is (    ).

    A. 夏　　　B. 戏　　　C. 鲜　　　D. 网　　　E. 腿

03) The LEGs are parts of the body that can move forwards and backwards. LEG is (    ).

    A. 腿　　　B. 闻　　　C. 夏　　　D. 文　　　E. 碗

04) The earliest Chinese CHARACTERs were usually engraved on the surface of hard objects, so the strokes were mostly straight lines. CHARACTER is (    ).

    A. 物　　　B. 忘　　　C. 碗　　　D. 文　　　E. 夏

05) Ancient BOWLs were made from stone. People used to kneel and be thankful when they had food to eat. BOWL is (    ).

    A. 闻　　　B. 碗　　　C. 位　　　D. 万　　　E. 忘

06) If you put your ear to the door you can HEAR what your neighbours are saying. HEAR is (    ).

    A. 物　　　B. 文　　　C. 闻　　　D. 戏　　　E. 腿

07) "卍" was an ancient holy symbol of Indian Buddhism which was introduced into China and changed into TEN THOUSAND, indicating the large number in the numeral system. TEN THOUSAND is (    ).

    A. 忘　　　B. 闻　　　C. 鲜　　　D. 碗　　　E. 万

08) Everything in the world, whether alive or inanimate, is called "MATTER". MATTER/THING is (    ).

    A. 戏　　　B. 碗　　　C. 忘　　　D. 物　　　E. 位

09) On a hot SUMMER day, it's best to wear a hat and have something that can cool you down. SUMMER is (    ).

    A. 夏　　　B. 戏　　　C. 网　　　D. 文　　　E. 碗

10) If something escapes from the heart, it can be called FORGETting. FORGET is (    ).

练习 Lesson 18

A. 戏　　B. 忘　　C. 鲜　　D. 物　　E. 腿

11) Weapons, painted faces, silk fans and gongs are all necessary things in a Chinese DRAMA. DRAMA is (　　).

A. 文　　B. 忘　　C. 万　　D. 鲜　　E. 戏

12) This character looks like the NET of a football match. NET is (　　).

A. 物　　B. 网　　C. 碗　　D. 鲜　　E. 夏

2. Match the character with the correct pronunciation.

夏　腿　文　鲜　碗　闻　忘　物　万　戏　网　位

xiān　wǎn　xià　xì　wàn　wén　wǎng　wèi　wén　tuǐ　wù　wàng

3. Draw the correct tone above each Chinese character OR write a number 0-4 to indicate the tone of each character.

01) 腿_____　02) 网_____　03) 夏_____　04) 闻_____

05) 碗_____　06) 戏_____　07) 物_____　08) 万_____

09) 忘_____　10) 鲜_____　11) 位_____　12) 文_____

4. Listen to the audio recording and choose the Chinese characters you hear.

01) _____　02) _____　03) _____　04) _____

05) _____　06) _____　07) _____　08) _____

09) _____　10) _____　11) _____　12) _____

A. 碗　　B. 腿　　C. 物　　D. 网　　E. 闻　　F. 忘
G. 万　　H. 位　　I. 戏　　J. 鲜　　K. 文　　L. 夏

5. Listen to the audio recording and write what you hear in Chinese characters.

01) _____　02) _____　03) _____　04) _____

05) _____　06) _____　07) _____　08) _____

09) _____　10) _____　11) _____　12) _____

6. Listen to the recording and write what you hear in Chinese characters.

01) _____　02) _____　03) _____　04) _____

05) _____　06) _____　07) _____　08) _____

09) _____　10) _____　11) _____　12) _____

7. **Translate the following sentences into English. (If there are characters in Chinese sentences that have not been learned, please check them in the "Character List" of the book.)**

01) 现在网上的新闻成千上万，文化少而又少，所以我不大看网站上的东西。

_____

02) 这出戏真新鲜，虽然我坐做的位子不怎么好，可是戏很好看。

_____

03) 那家饭馆儿的老板是个新闻人物，我忘了他的名字了。夏天的时候，这位老板上过几次电视。他饭馆儿的菜很新鲜，每次我都会要一小碗火腿，鲜得不得了。

_____

# Lesson 19  569–580  相、香、箱、响、向、像、鞋、心、信、熊、须、需

**1. Circle the correct character according to the all-caps word in each catchphrase.**

01) This building is very warm because the windows face TOWARDS the sun. TOWARDS is (    ).

   A. 须     B. 相     C. 鞋     D. 向     E. 信

02) The people living in this desert house really NEED some rain. NEED is (    ).

   A. 熊     B. 需     C. 鞋     D. 心     E. 像

03) The wind blows this man's long BEARD from his face. BEARD is (    ).

   A. 像     B. 熊     C. 箱     D. 向     E. 须

04) A pair of eyes flashed from inside the tree, SEEing and taking PICTURES of the outside world. SEE/EACH OTHER/PICTURE is (    ).

   A. 需     B. 相     C. 信     D. 香     E. 响

05) My neighbour and I yelled at one another with a loud SOUND. SOUND is (    ).

   A. 响     B. 像     C. 香     D. 信     E. 须

06) A man finds some buried bones which assemble into the IMAGE of an ancient elephant. IMAGE is (    ).

   A. 信     B. 像     C. 鞋     D. 相     E. 心

07) Making corn into popcorn really tastes DELICIOUS! DELICIOUS is (    ).

   A. 香     B. 向     C. 熊     D. 须     E. 箱

08) The character for heart looks like an actual HEART. HEART is (    ).

   A. 向     B. 鞋     C. 须     D. 信     E. 心

09) Ancient people would use stones to cut leather to make simple SHOEs. SHOE is (    ).

   A. 须     B. 香     C. 响     D. 鞋     E. 相

10) See the bamboo BOX in the middle of the jungle? BOX/CASE is (    )

   A. 鞋     B. 箱     C. 心     D. 熊     E. 须

11) Once language is recorded, it becomes a testimony of TRUST. TRUST is (    ).

   A. 响     B. 箱     C. 信     D. 像     E. 心

12) The combined characters of head, body and claws form the character for BEAR. BEAR is (    ).

A. 熊    B. 向    C. 响    D. 需    E. 须

**2. Match the character with the correct pronunciation.**

须　心　响　向　相　熊　鞋　箱　需　香　像　信

xīn　xū　xiāng　xiàng　xìn　xióng　xū　xiǎng　xiāng　xié　xiàng　xiāng/xiàng

**3. Draw the correct tone above each Chinese character OR write a number 0-4 to indicate the tone of each character.**

01) 须_____　02) 心_____　03) 鞋_____　04) 香_____
05) 需_____　06) 箱_____　07) 像_____　08) 相_____
09) 熊_____　10) 响_____　11) 向_____　12) 信_____

**4. Listen to the audio recording and choose the Chinese characters you hear.**

01) _____　02) _____　03) _____　04) _____
05) _____　06) _____　07) _____　08) _____
09) _____　10) _____　11) _____　12) _____

A. 需　　B. 响　　C. 鞋　　D. 像　　E. 信　　F. 心
G. 箱　　H. 香　　I. 须　　J. 向　　K. 相　　L. 熊

**5. Listen to the audio recording and write what you hear in Chinese characters.**

01) _____　02) _____　03) _____　04) _____
05) _____　06) _____　07) _____　08) _____
09) _____　10) _____　11) _____　12) _____

**6. Listen to the recording and write what you hear in Chinese characters.**

01) _____　02) _____　03) _____　04) _____
05) _____　06) _____　07) _____　08) _____
09) _____　10) _____　11) _____　12) _____

**7. Translate the following sentences into English. (If there are characters in Chinese sentences that have not been learned, please check them in the "Character List" of the book.)**

01) 我有**信心**向你说，我买的**鞋相信**没有问题，一定不大不小。

02) 这个音**箱**的音**响**很好，不**需**要再换其他的了。

03) 现在北极的白**熊必须**也**像熊**猫一样得到世界的关爱。

04) 我的房子面**向**南，很亮，而且院子也大，一到夏天，鸟语花**香**，住在这里真的非常理想。

# Lesson 20  581–592 选、牙、阳、爷、业、姨、议、易、音、银、饮、应

**1. Circle the correct character according to the all-caps word in each catchphrase.**

01) This thin man examines all his food and wine, looking for something to DRINK. DRINK is (    ).

   A. 业　　　B. 牙　　　C. 爷　　　D. 饮　　　E. 应

02) MUSIC begins from the heart below and comes out through expression. MUSIC is (    ).

   A. 音　　　B. 饮　　　C. 银　　　D. 易　　　E. 阳

03) Gold and SILVER are both precious metals, but silver is not as valuable as gold. SILVER is (    ).

   A. 易　　　B. 应　　　C. 姨　　　D. 业　　　E. 银

04) The tiny bird on the rooftop calls out to his three friends across the street but they do not RESPOND. SHOULD/RESPOND is (    ).

   A. 选　　　B. 牙　　　C. 应　　　D. 议　　　E. 银

05) The character for CHANGE shows the positive sun atop the negative shadow in a continuous cycle. CHANGE is (    ).

   A. 阳　　　B. 易　　　C. 姨　　　D. 业　　　E. 音

06) The gaps between TEETH need to be brushed frequently to keep healthy. TEETH is (    ).

   A. 牙　　　B. 选　　　C. 姨　　　D. 爷　　　E. 饮

07) This runner was first to cross the finish line and was SELECTed for the finals. SELECT is (    ).

   A. 阳　　　B. 姨　　　C. 业　　　D. 选　　　E. 易

08) Many people must DISCUSS an idea before raising their hands for a final vote. DISCUSS is (    ).

   A. 姨　　　B. 业　　　C. 饮　　　D. 爷　　　E. 议

09) In this picture, father below bows to his father above, my GRANDFATHER. GRANDFATHER is (    ).

   A. 选　　　B. 爷　　　C. 音　　　D. 银　　　E. 易

10) The hot SUN shines brightly on the cliff. SUN is (    ).

   A. 阳　　　B. 业　　　C. 银　　　D. 应　　　E. 饮

练习 Lesson 20

11) My AUNT loves to wear funny styles of clothing. AUNT is ( ).

A. 议　　　B. 爷　　　C. 姨　　　D. 应　　　E. 易

12) This character for LINE OF BUSINESS shows two workers together. It is mostly used as a suffix element of business/industry/occupation. LINE OF BUSINESS is ( ).

A. 应　　　B. 音　　　C. 业　　　D. 易　　　E. 牙

2. Match the character with the correct pronunciation.

银　饮　音　阳　业　选　姨　爷　牙　易　应　议

yīn　yīng/yìng　yì　yáng　xuǎn　yì　yí　yín　yé　yá　yè　yǐn

3. Draw the correct tone above each Chinese character OR write a number 0-4 to indicate the tone of each character.

01) 饮_____　02) 银_____　03) 牙_____　04) 姨_____

05) 爷_____　06) 音_____　07) 选_____　08) 易_____

09) 业_____　10) 应_____　11) 阳_____　12) 议_____

4. Listen to the audio recording and choose the Chinese characters you hear.

01) _____　02) _____　03) _____　04) _____

05) _____　06) _____　07) _____　08) _____

09) _____　10) _____　11) _____　12) _____

A. 银　　B. 牙　　C. 议　　D. 选　　E. 应　　F. 阳

G. 饮　　H. 姨　　I. 爷　　J. 易　　K. 业　　L. 音

5. Listen to the audio recording and write what you hear in Chinese characters.

01) _____　02) _____　03) _____　04) _____

05) _____　06) _____　07) _____　08) _____

09) _____　10) _____　11) _____　12) _____

6. Listen to the recording and write what you hear in Chinese characters.

01) _____　02) _____　03) _____　04) _____

05) _____　06) _____　07) _____　08) _____

09) _____　10) _____　11) _____　12) _____

7. **Translate the following sentences into English. (If there are characters in Chinese sentences that have not been learned, please check them in the "Character List" of the book.)**

01) 我这回给你姨妈选的音乐特别有阳刚气，她一定会喜欢。

02) 我爷爷都九十九岁了，虽然他的眼睛不好，可是牙还不错，他一生在银行业做了五十年！

03) 我们昨天商议好的，也是你答应的：我们的分工是你做容易的事——去买饮料，我来做不那么容易的事——做饭。好，我们现在开始吧！

# Lesson 21  593–604 迎、用、邮、又、于、育、遇、元、园、愿、越、澡

1. **Circle the correct character according to the all-caps word in each catchphrase.**

01) A mother must do her best to RAISE her baby. RAISE is (   ).
   A. 元    B. 育    C. 迎    D. 用    E. 越

02) Two people stop and MEET on a farmland road. MEET is (   ).
   A. 育    B. 又    C. 澡    D. 于    E. 遇

03) I am neither AT the T-junction nor at the crossroads. I am at the bottom of this vertical line. AT is (   ).
   A. 于    B. 澡    C. 愿    D. 遇    E. 越

04) When people walk into your home, the tradition is to be polite and cordially WELCOME them. WELCOME is (   ).
   A. 越    B. 澡    C. 邮    D. 迎    E. 愿

05) This tree is having a bubble BATH in the rainwater. BATH is (   ).
   A. 迎    B. 邮    C. 园    D. 澡    E. 遇

06) A shelf unit with partitions is very USEful! USE is (   ).
   A. 用    B. 邮    C. 迎    D. 元    E. 越

07) Combining the characters for father and mother on top, and child beneath, we create the word for ORIGIN. ORIGIN is (   ).
   A. 元    B. 迎    C. 用    D. 愿    E. 园

08) POSTal mail can pass through cities, towns, and the countryside. POST is (   ).
   A. 越    B. 又    C. 园    D. 育    E. 邮

09) This climber is well-prepared with all of his tools. He will surely SURPASS all the others. SURPASS is (   ).
   A. 越    B. 愿    C. 育    D. 邮    E. 于

10) A PARK is a unit of land with trees, flowers, paths, and all the elements of life surrounded by walls. GARDEN/PARK is (   ).
   A. 用    B. 园    C. 育    D. 遇    E. 澡

11) The picture shows three fingers, which means that number one is odd, number two is even, and number three AGAIN is also odd. AGAIN is (   ).
   A. 邮    B. 迎    C. 越    D. 又    E. 愿

12) A WISH has its origin in the heart before it is expressed. WISH is (   ).

A. 迎　　　B. 愿　　　C. 于　　　D. 园　　　E. 育

**2. Match the character with the correct pronunciation.**

澡　又　元　用　愿　越　邮　遇　育　园　于　迎

yuán　yù　yuè　yòu　yú　yóu　yòng　yù　yíng　zǎo　yuán　yuàn

**3. Draw the correct tone above each Chinese character OR write a number 0-4 to indicate the tone of each character.**

01) 用_____　02) 澡_____　03) 元_____　04) 愿_____

05) 越_____　06) 遇_____　07) 育_____　08) 于_____

09) 园_____　10) 邮_____　11) 迎_____　12) 又_____

**4. Listen to the audio recording and choose the Chinese characters you hear.**

01) _____　02) _____　03) _____　04) _____

05) _____　06) _____　07) _____　08) _____

09) _____　10) _____　11) _____　12) _____

A. 越　　B. 愿　　C. 于　　D. 园　　E. 育　　F. 澡

G. 迎　　H. 遇　　I. 邮　　J. 元　　K. 又　　L. 用

**5. Listen to the audio recording and write what you hear in Chinese characters.**

01) _____　02) _____　03) _____　04) _____

05) _____　06) _____　07) _____　08) _____

09) _____　10) _____　11) _____　12) _____

**6. Listen to the recording and write what you hear in Chinese characters.**

01) _____　02) _____　03) _____　04) _____

05) _____　06) _____　07) _____　08) _____

09) _____　10) _____　11) _____　12) _____

**7. Translate the following sentences into English. (If there are characters in Chinese sentences that have not been learned, please check them in the "Character List" of the book.)**

01) 你等我半个小时好吗？我洗了**澡**就去**迎**你。

02) 现在大家都**愿**意**用**电**邮**，或者更喜欢**用**手机发短信，**用**笔写信的**越**来**越**少了。因为手机**又**快**又**方便。

---

03) 我昨天在公**园遇**到了一个原来在教**育**学院读书的同学，他告诉我他**于**今年**元**月在西班牙定居了。

---

## Lesson 22  605–618 择、张、照、者、直、终、种、重、周、主、注、自、总、嘴

**1. Circle the correct character according to the all-caps word in each catchphrase.**

01) This is a four-story building that goes STRAIGHT up and down. STRAIGHT is (    ).

   A. 直    B. 择    C. 照    D. 注    E. 终

02) The well below supplies water to the SURROUNDING farmland and vegetable fields. SURROUNDING is (    ).

   A. 周    B. 重    C. 张    D. 注    E. 自

03) Behind this painted Peking opera mask is the PERSON. PERSON is (    ).

   A. 择    B. 周    C. 嘴    D. 者    E. 自

04) This rectangular billboard is very HEAVY and needs to be firmly fixed both at its top and the bottom. HEAVY/REPEAT is (    ).

   A. 直    B. 终    C. 择    D. 重    E. 主

05) It's a pity that just as I finished sewing my woolly hat, winter WAS OVER. BE OVER is (    ).

   A. 照    B. 终    C. 嘴    D. 总    E. 自

06) This character represents a nose. Chinese people often point to their nose when referring to THEMSELVES. ONESELF is (    ).

   A. 注    B. 自    C. 照    D. 择    E. 张

07) SEEDs should be PLANTed in the middle of the hole. SEED/PLANT is (    ).

   A. 者    B. 注    C. 嘴    D. 择    E. 种

08) First you must CHOOSE with your mind, and then select with your hand. CHOOSE is (    ).

   A. 照    B. 直    C. 终    D. 择    E. 重

09) This bow can BE OPENED so far that it can unleash five arrows at a time. BE OPENED is (    ).

   A. 重    B. 择    C. 张    D. 注    E. 总

10) Cars on secondary roads should give way to cars on the MAIN road. MAIN/MASTER is (    ).

   A. 择    B. 自    C. 种    D. 主    E. 周

11) Pay ATTENTION and watch out for crocodiles which inhabit the main waters

around here. ATTENTION is ( ).

    A. 周      B. 注      C. 者      D. 择      E. 主

12) When entering a dangerous place, you need to ILLUMINATE the area with a torch and hold a weapon for self-defense. ILLUMINATE is ( ).

    A. 照      B. 择      C. 终      D. 自      E. 重

13) Your MOUTH will quickly alert you if there is something hard or sharp in what you are about to eat. MOUTH is ( ).

    A. 嘴      B. 总      C. 主      D. 者      E. 自

14) To SUM UP my results into a decision, I must consider the thoughts of my brain and the feelings from my heart. SUM UP is ( ).

    A. 照      B. 总      C. 终      D. 自      E. 重

**2. Match the character with the correct pronunciation.**

自    周    注    择    种    直    重    终    张    者    照    主    嘴    总

zhí  zhǒng/zhòng  zhě  zhǔ  zhōng  zhāng  zé  zhào  zhōu  zhù  zì  zhòng/chóng  zuǐ  zǒng

**3. Draw the correct tone above each Chinese character OR write a number 0-4 to indicate the tone of each character.**

01) 主_____    02) 直_____    03) 自_____    04) 者_____

05) 张_____    06) 种_____    07) 择_____    08) 周_____

09) 照_____    10) 注_____    11) 终_____    12) 重_____

13) 嘴_____    14) 总_____

**4. Listen to the audio recording and choose the Chinese characters you hear.**

01) _____    02) _____    03) _____    04) _____

05) _____    06) _____    07) _____    08) _____

09) _____    10) _____    11) _____    12) _____

13) _____    14) _____

A. 自    B. 注    C. 主    D. 周    E. 择    F. 直    G. 种

H. 照    I. 终    J. 重    K. 张    L. 者    M. 总    N. 嘴

**5. Listen to the audio recording and write what you hear in Chinese characters.**

01) _____    02) _____    03) _____    04) _____

05) _____  06) _____  07) _____  08) _____
09) _____  10) _____  11) _____  12) _____
13) _____  14) _____

**6. Listen to the recording and write what you hear in Chinese characters.**

01) _____  02) _____  03) _____  04) _____
05) _____  06) _____  07) _____  08) _____
09) _____  10) _____  11) _____  12) _____
13) _____  14) _____

**7. Translate the following sentences into English. (If there are characters in Chinese sentences that have not been learned, please check them in the "Character List" of the book.)**

01) 我爸爸不但**主张**在园子里**种**花、**种**树，而且还很注意选**择**花的颜色和树**种**，不能有太高的树，不然花得不到日**照**会长不好。

_____

02) **总**的来说，我自己一**直**很喜欢那位报新闻的记**者**，她的**嘴**很能说。这**周**有她的一个节目，叫《月末年**终**》，我得去听听。

_____

03) 在这些**照**片里我选**择**这十几**张**，主要是**照**片的作**者**选**择**的题目很**重**要，而且他**照**的东西一点都不**重**复，**张张**都有新鲜感。

_____

# Lesson 23  349–360 阿、啊、矮、安、把、般、搬、板、办、半、包、饱

**All the exercises below are based on the combinations and phrases containing Characters** 阿，啊，矮，安，把，般，搬，板，办，半，包 and 饱.

1. Translate the following sentences into English.

01）好漂亮的鲜花啊！是给我的吗？

02）阿姨上星期搬家了，搬到城西，离我家有五站路远。

03）我们三个人长得就如同姐妹一般，高矮胖瘦都差不多。

04）每当我练字时，阿姨总是安静地坐在旁边，认真地为我把关。

05）五年级的教室里安静极了，一点儿动静也没有。

06）山上的空气好，爷爷奶奶在那儿住了个把月，都不想回到城市里来了。

07）一般来说，在我们公司新人的试用期是三个月。

08）爷爷家的地板已经很旧了，可他还是不愿意换新的。

09）三楼有一间空着的办公室，要不你们先用那间？

10）这大半年他一直在周游世界，从北半球到南半球，去了不少地方。

11）每天早上我都会在公司旁边的咖啡馆儿里喝一杯咖啡，吃两片面包。

12）这次的一级种子比上次的饱满多了。

2. Translate the following sentences into Chinese.

01) My aunt is flying to Beijing tomorrow.
_____

02) He is very inflexible.
_____

03) Whose school bag is this?
_____

04) She is very short, therefore she always wears high heels.
_____

05) The teacher wrote down the name list on the blackboard.
_____

06) This table is too heavy to move by myself.
_____

07) Everyone reads quietly in the library.
_____

08) I will try to find a way to solve this problem.
_____

09) I ate two buns and I'm full now.
_____

10) Shall we split this cake half and half?
_____

3. Listen, translate and repeat the recorded sentences.

*For example:*
*Step one: Listen to the sentence.*
   the first time "我爸爸是老师。"
   the second time "我爸爸是老师。"
*Step two: Translate.*
   / My dad is a teacher.
*Step three: Listen again.*
   the third time "我爸爸是老师。"
*Step four: Repeat the sentence.*
   "我爸爸是老师。"

01) 我**阿姨**是网球教练。

02) 好甜的苹果**啊**！你**把**这两个都吃了吧，吃**半饱**也不错啊！

03) 他们一家人都很**矮**小。

04) 你什么时候**搬**家？

05) 我才不会和他一**般**见识呢。

06) 黑**板**上的字太小了，我看不清楚。

07) 带上个大**包**这**办**法不错。

08) 午休时**办**公室里一个人都没有，**安静**极了。

# Lesson 24  361–372 被、鼻、必、变、冰、才、参、草、层、查、差、尝

All the exercises below are based on the combinations and phrases containing characters 被, 鼻, 必, 变, 冰, 才, 参, 草, 层, 查, 差 and 尝.

1. Translate the following sentences into English.

01) 哥哥最喜爱的游戏机被我一不小心打坏了。
___

02) 你把我的鼻子画得又大又难看。
___

03) 根据地图来看，我们必须在下个车站换车去黄山。
___

04) 我们有五年没见了，你变化真大，变得我都认不出来了。
___

05) 我家的冰箱坏了，里面的东西都化了。
___

06) 我和查小刚中午见面聊了三个多小时，刚刚才分手。
___

07) 李老师也报名参加学校一年一次的网球比赛了。
___

08) 我平时不爱打理花园里的那些花花草草，一般都是我丈夫打理。
___

09) 我姐姐说她家的那层楼里住着一位有名的歌唱家。
___

10) 出门前他把自己要带的行李检查了一遍又一遍才放了心。
___

11) 你和他差远了，他七岁时就在市里比赛得第一了。
___

12) 快来尝尝妈妈刚刚做好的红烧肉，可好吃了。
___

练习　Lesson 24

2. Translate the following sentences into Chinese.

01) We are all touched by his story.

02) My nose really hurts.

03) You must get there by eight o'clock tomorrow morning.

04) Do you know there are new changes in the train timetable?

05) This fridge is too big to move into that room.

06) I have just been to the supermarket.

07) Do you want to take part in this competition?

08) This decision is made by the company's top management, I am so happy!

09) The ticket officer is checking everyone's ticket.

10) Do you want to try this fresh green tea?

3. Listen, translate and repeat the recorded sentences.

01) 我被她的歌声打动了。

02) 他感冒了，鼻子不通，尝不出这个菜的好坏。

03) 天气变冷，水都结冰了。

04）你**必须**做完作业**才**能出去**参**加比赛。

05）三个多月没下雨，**草**地都黄了。

06）他**查**看了一下自己的笔记本。

07）商场的七层新开了一家电影院。

08）这两个孩子**差**不多大。

# Lesson 25  373–385 超、衬、成、城、迟、除、楚、船、春、词、聪、答、带

**All the exercises below are based on the combinations and phrases containing characters** 超,衬,成,城,迟,除,楚,船,春,词,聪,答 **and** 带.

1. Translate the following sentences into English.

01) 商场的一楼新开了一家超市，卖的都是从西班牙进口的水果。

02) 这件白衬衫你已经穿了很久了，再买件新的吧。

03) 经过努力，弟弟这学期的数学成绩有了很大的进步。

04) 这几年来城市里的绿化不但越来越多，也越来越好了。

05) 对于她老是迟到，我已经习惯了。

06) 那条山路除了他，我们谁都没走过。

07) 我近视，坐在后面根本看不清楚老师在黑板上写的字。

08) 你们是打算坐船还是坐飞机去日本？

09) 为了学好法文，我买了好几本中法词典。

10) 在学习方面，他是我认识的最聪明的人。

11) 你能让我回去想一想再回答你吗？

12) 上星期天我带妹妹去动物园看大熊猫了。

13) 春回大地，是一年中最好的季节。

2. Translate the following sentences into Chinese.

01) Do you usually shop at the supermarket?

02) I just bought two new shirts; one is green, the other is blue.

03) We can finish this job on time.

04) Are there any universities in this city?

05) He will come sooner or later.

06) Nobody can help him except himself.

07) I'm still not clear what you want.

08) They went back to live on a boat again at the beginning of spring.

09) Where is your (word) dictionary?

10) He answered the boss's question clearly.

3. Listen, translate and repeat the recorded sentences.

01) 我把我新做**成**的红衬衫借给她了。

02) 他干的坏事我一清二**楚**。

03) 你明天上学别**迟**到，**除**了词典，还有数学书都带着。

04) 我上班的公司在**城北**。

05）你真**聪**明，我刚说你就明白了。

06）她**答**应今天上午十点钟到**超**市去。

07）他会**带**着妻子一起来参加**春**节晚会。

08）爸爸买了下周二去南平的**船**票。

# Lesson 26  386–397 单、担、当、灯、地、典、定、冬、短、段、锻、朵

All the exercises below are based on the combinations and phrases containing characters 单, 担, 当, 灯, 地, 典, 定, 冬, 短, 段, 锻 and 朵.

1. Translate the following sentences into English.

01) 她看了看菜**单**，点了两个最贵的菜和一瓶红酒。

02) 雪下得这么大，妈妈非常**担**心爸爸开车回家。

03) **短**跑是我最拿手的体育运动。

04) 姐姐静静**地**坐在那儿，一边看书一边听音乐。

05) **冬**天了，才下午三点，路边的街**灯**就亮起来了。

06) 对我来说这本新词**典**相**当**有用。

07) 他思前想后，最后还是决**定**离开公司，做出国留学的准备。

08) 北方的**冬**天很冷，经常下大雪。

09) 妹妹一下飞机就给妈妈发了一个**短**信。

10) 最近怎么没见你来体育中心**锻**炼身体？是不是工作太忙了？

11) 那天在婚礼的会场上放了一**段**他们相识的**短**片。

12) 爷爷耳**朵**不好，所以讲话的声音很大。

练习 Lesson 26

2. Translate the following sentences into Chinese.

01) Can I have the menu please?

02) I was afraid that you wouldn't come.

03) There are many different coloured flowers in my garden.

04) Of course, you can use my dictionary.

05) She is singing happily.

06) I decide to go swimming this afternoon.

07) Do you like winter sports?

08) Your skirt is too short.

09) He goes to the gym to exercise twice a week.

10) The lights in his room are on all night.

3. Listen, translate and repeat the recorded sentences.

01) 她已经**单**身好几年了。

02) 他一直帮妈妈分**担**家务。

03) **当**地人对游客一向很热情。

04) 客房的**灯**不亮了。

05）下班了，他为了**锻**炼身体，慢慢地走回了家。
_____

06）这**段**经**典**的**短**文《一**朵**小红花》是张老师写的。
_____

07）你喜欢的东西不一**定**是我喜欢的。
_____

08）北方的**冬**天又刮风又下雪，真冷！
_____

# Lesson 27  398–409 饿、而、耳、发、法、方、放、风、附、复、该、干

**All the exercises below are based on the combinations and phrases containing characters** 饿, 而, 耳, 发, 法, 方, 放, 风, 附, 复, 该 **and** 干.

1. Translate the following sentences into English.

01) 一进家门就闻到了饭菜的香，我突然觉得好**饿**。

02) 周老师不但会说**法**语，**而**且还会说西班牙语。

03) 老师讲得有声有色，可我一**耳**朵都没听进去。

04) 车子在半道上走不动了，他检查了半天，什么也没**发**现，只能打电话给车行。

05) 这两个**方法**你觉得哪一个比较好？

06) 弟弟非常调皮，我拿他一点儿办**法**都没有。

07) 上个周末又是刮**风**又是下雨，我哪儿都没去，一直在家看书。

08) 女儿已经十八岁了，还不会好好照顾自己，实在让我不**放**心。

09) 我表弟的大学实现了电子化，学生的作业可以用电子邮件**附**件**发**给老师了。

10) 一到考试期间图书馆里就坐满了忙着**复**习的学生。

11) 一般来说，晚上七点以后我应**该**都在家。

12) 这些杯子都是**干**净的，妈妈早上才洗过。

2. Translate the following sentences into Chinese.

01) What's for dinner? I'm starving.

02) This dish doesn't just look good, it is also very tasty.

03) Have you seen my white headphone?

04) I've used a lot of methods, but I can't find anything wrong with your computer.

05) I don't believe she would do that.

06) It's very windy today.

07) You rest assured that I will look after your cat.

08) Is there a coffee shop nearby?

09) Can you repeat that one more time?

10) You should be more serious about your work.

3. Listen, translate and repeat the recorded sentences.

01) **饿**的时候吃什么都觉得香。

02) 姐姐不但长得漂亮**而且**聪明。

03) 新出的游戏让我**耳目一新**。

04) 你有解决这个问题的**方法**吗？

05）我的帽子被风刮走了。

06）你平安到家了发短信给我，我才能放心。

07）他总是重复着说同样的话。

08）你应该多帮妈妈干点儿家务，附带着做早饭。

# Lesson 28  410–421 感、刚、糕、根、跟、更、故、顾、刮、怪、惯、害

**All the exercises below are based on the combinations and phrases containing characters** 感, 刚, 糕, 根, 跟, 更, 故, 顾, 刮, 怪, 惯 **and** 害.

1. Translate the following sentences into English.

01) 笑笑的**感**冒已经好得差不多了，明天可以去上班了。

02) 医生**刚**才来过了，给奶奶做完检查就走了。

03) 每次路过街口的那家蛋**糕**店，哥哥都会进去买几块蛋**糕**。

04) **根**据你的要求，我会给你留一个走道旁边的位子。

05) 姐姐穿的那条裙子让她看上去**更**瘦了。

06) 这个**故**事的情节十分简单。

07) 这家饭馆儿开张没多久，就已经有很多**顾**客了。

08) 叔叔的成就让很多人对他**刮**目相看。

09) 我非常奇**怪**会在这儿遇见你们。

10) 别担心，你很快就会习**惯**这里的天气。

11) 他的狗在前面走，他在后面**跟**着。

12) 天气这么冷，我很**害**怕自己会生病。

练习 Lesson 28

2. Translate the following sentences into Chinese.

01) Do you have any cold medicine?

02) He was here a moment ago. I don't know where he is now.

03) Who made this cake?

04) According to the news on TV, tomorrow will be a windy day.

05) I always drive more carefully at night.

06) I read this story in the newspaper last year.

07) There is not a single customer this morning.

08) In north China, it is often windy in spring.

09) I am surprised that he did not come.

10) She is not used to drinking beer at night.

3. Listen, translate and repeat the recorded sentences.

01）我妈妈跟阿姨都感冒得很厉害。

02）你刚才讲的我都同意。

03）姐姐不但爱吃蛋糕也会做蛋糕。

04）他这样做是故意的，我的担心不是没有根据的。

05）我们的城市需要**更**多的绿化。
___

06）**刮**大风了，你放心吧，我会照**顾**好你的小狗。
___

07）她有一个很奇**怪**的愿望。
___

08）我不习**惯**这么早起床。
___

# Lesson 29  422–233 行、河、乎、护、花、化、画、坏、环、换、黄、婚

**All the exercises below are based on the combinations and phrases containing characters** 行, 河, 乎, 护, 花, 化, 画, 坏, 环, 换, 黄 **and** 婚.

1. Translate the following sentences into English.

01) 这个**行**李箱太大了，把它放到汽车后面的**行**李箱里吧。

02) **黄河**是中国的第二大**河**。

03) 高老师给了那位学生几**乎**是满分的成绩。

04) 你把**护**照带上了吧？

05) 这些黄色的**花**朵很好看，可它们没有香气。

06) 他在大学学东方国家的文**化**。

07) 这个正在**画画**儿的女孩子真漂亮。

08) 比赛能不能进**行**，要看天气的好**坏**。

09) 她现在心情不好，**换**个**环**境对她会好一些。

10) 你能告诉我你的这对耳**环**是在哪儿买的吗？

11) 这菜单里的菜能变**换**一下吗？我们不喜欢老吃同样的东西。

12) 听说小奇要结**婚**了？什么时候办**婚**礼？

2. Translate the following sentences into Chinese.

01) Why is your suitcase so heavy?

02) We could hardly believe our eyes.

03) She can't find her passport.

04) The Sunday flower market sells all sorts of flowers.

05) We are aware that the market has changed.

06) This is a freehand sketch.

07) She had at last found an ideal environment.

08) My car broken down, so I have to take the bus now.

09) He is very interested in Chinese culture.

10) It was a happy wedding.

3. Listen, translate and repeat the recorded sentences.

01) 爸爸的行李箱坏了，得换个新的。

02) 他不在乎在美化环境上花钱。

03) 每个人都应该爱护自然环境。

04) 这种花儿的开花期是六月到九月。

05）画水彩人物头像她很拿手。

06）她很喜欢现在黄河边的新环境。

07）我的手表怎么坏了？

08）你们婚礼的日期决定了吗？

# Lesson 30  434–447 或, 级, 极, 急, 己, 记, 季, 绩, 加, 假, 检, 简, 健, 讲

**All the exercises below are based on the combinations and phrases from characters** 或, 级, 极, 急, 己, 记, 季, 绩, 加, 假, 检, 简, 健 **and** 讲.

1. Translate the following sentences into English.

01) 花园后面的那块空地我们可以用于种菜**或**者种花。

02) 她的工作成**绩**远比其他人好。

03) 看见马可欢在哭，我感到难过**极**了。

04) 这点小事你怎么就**急**成那个样子了。

05) 你忘**记**打电话了，她会生气吗？

06) 工人们在为雨**季**的到来做准备。

07) 我不知道穿什么样的服去参**加**明天的晚会好。

08) 下个星期我有三天的**假**期，我们去哪儿玩儿？

09) 他已经把**检**查的结果用邮件发给了经理。

10) 这件事看上去**简**单，但是做起来不**简**单呢！

11) 新鲜的空气对**健**康很重要。

12) 他妻子很爱说话，一有机会就**讲**个没完。

13) 王先生在公司**级**别很高，可他的穿着很一般。

14）这层楼的房子不是我自己的，是我奶奶的。

2. Translate the following sentences into Chinese.

01) You can wear an evening dress or skirt to the party.

02) He is very anxious about his exam results.

03) She was so pleased when she saw her present.

04) I was anxious before the exam as I was worried that I wouldn't pass the level test this time.

05) She probably forgot to tell him.

06) Can I have a season ticket please?

07) Only fifty people attended Mimi's wedding last Saturday.

08) The manager gave the staff the day off.

09) You had better have a physical check-up.

10) It's remarkable that he's made such a big progress.

3. Listen, translate and repeat the recorded sentences.

01）妈妈检查了一下，小明的学习成绩是中等。

02）她穿着一条绿色的裙子，漂亮极了。

03）今天不知他怎么了，没讲上几句话他就**急**了。

04）我很**健**忘，只**记**得他是三年**级或**者二年**级**的学生，可是名字忘了。

05）一年四**季**中，妈妈最喜欢秋**季**。

06）弟弟非常想报名参**加**网球课。

07）他请了一个月的**假**去西安玩儿。

08）今天的晚饭比较**简**单。因为都是自**己**人。

# Lesson 31  448–459 蕉、角、脚、较、接、街、节、结、解、界、借、斤

**All the exercises below are based on the combinations and phrases containing characters** 蕉, 角, 脚, 较, 接, 街, 节, 结, 解, 界, 借 **and** 斤.

1. Translate the following sentences into English.

01) 香**蕉**是一种很常见的水果，大**街**上哪儿都有卖的。

02) 他站在街**角**，一边听着音乐，一边在等他的女朋友。

03) 她唱着歌，**脚**步轻快地下楼去了。

04) 足球和篮球比**较**起来，打篮球我更拿手。

05) 从上个星期到**接**下来的几个星期，哥哥忙得都没时间睡觉。

06) 我们走了两条**街**才找到一辆开往市中心的出租车。

07) 被认为最有希望拿第一的人**结**果没被选上。

08) 这种桌椅可以根据孩子的身高调**节**。

09) 别着急，他们一定会很快**解**决这些问题。

10) 这次是您去周游世**界**的好机会，可别错过了。

11) 弟弟从图书馆里**借**了一本关于西方文化的书。

12) 阿姨生了一场大病，体重轻了十多**斤**。

2. Translate the following sentences into Chinese.

01) I like bananas and I also like apples. What about you?

02) She is the leading role in the play.

03) I heard footsteps outside.

04) She quite likes long distance running, but she doesn't like the high jump.

05) Here is an apple for you — catch!

06) When crossing the road, look out for cars.

07) The results of the competition are coming out.

08) What television program are you watching?

09) The difficult problem has not yet definitely been settled. It needs time.

10) The world is full of wonders.

3. Listen, translate and repeat the recorded sentences.

01) 请问香蕉多少钱一斤？

02) 他们三个人加快了脚步往前走。

03) 球虽然出界了，可是有了一个比较好的角球机会。

04）妹妹感冒了，**接**着又发烧了。

05）她在**街**对面大声地叫你呢！

06）周叔叔下个月要**结**婚了。

07）五、六月是百花开放的季**节**，我们**借**一辆车出去玩儿好吗？

08）你有**解**决这个问题的办法吗？

# Lesson 32   460–471 净、静、境、久、酒、旧、居、句、据、决、卡、康

**All the exercises below are based on the combinations and phrases containing characters** 净，静，境，久，酒，旧，居，句，据，决，卡 and 康．

1. Translate the following sentences into English.

01) 买完菜回家后，妈妈把鱼和肉都洗干**净**了，然后放进了冰箱里。

02) 环**境**问题一直是这二十年来大家都很关注的话题。

03) 他那么安**静**，几乎没人注意到他在场。

04) 她花了很**久**的时间才写完这本小说。

05) 不到月末就没钱了，他只能怪自己喝**酒**花的钱太多了。

06) 搬家时姐姐把我们的一些**旧**家电都送给邻居了。

07) 妹妹到法国**居**住后很快就学会了法语。

08) 这些**句**子又短又简单，很容易听懂。

09) **据**说我们酒店不久就会来一位新经理。

10) 所有的人都知道，公司的这个**决**定会影响到三千员工的去留。

11) 我没带零钱，可以用信用**卡**吗？

12) 为了健**康**我一直在努力地锻炼身体。

练习 Lesson 32

2. Translate the following sentences into Chinese.

01）Have the stairs been swept clean?

02）Will you be quiet?

03）He stood there for a long time for meeting the manager.

04）Peter is not in the habit of drinking a lot as he thinks it would be bad for his health.

05）She uses the old iron box as a table.

06）My neighbour is a dentist.

07）She thought this sentence was very witty.

08）His fear was well founded.

09）She has finally determined to divorce with her husband.

10）This shop doesn't take credit cards.

3. Listen, translate and repeat the recorded sentences.

01）我把要带居住卡和健康卡的事情忘得一干二净，所以出得来，进不去了。

02）这里真安静啊！

03）阿姨不打算在北京久住。

04）她不喜欢没有下酒菜只喝酒。
_____

05）这只旧表是爷爷留给我的。
_____

06）不知为什么他看着我一句话也不说。
_____

07）你说这句话有什么根据吗？
_____

08）米米最后还是服从了她爸爸要她离境回国的决定。
_____

# Lesson 33  472–484 渴、刻、空、口、哭、裤、筷、蓝、礼、李、理、力、历

**All the exercises below are based on the combinations and phrases containing characters** 渴, 刻, 空, 口, 哭, 裤, 筷, 蓝, 礼, 李, 理, 力 **and** 历.

1. Translate the following sentences into English.

   01) 这么热的天气让人口**渴**得很。
   _____

   02) 我觉得又**渴**又累，还有点儿发烧。
   _____

   03) 现在的火车时**刻**表在网上也可以查到了。
   _____

   04) 天气这么热，你怎么不开**空**调？
   _____

   05) 他很爱／好面子，那种向朋友借钱的话，他实在说不出**口**。
   _____

   06) 弟弟回答老师问题的时候，声音像**哭**一样。
   _____

   07) 这条**裤**子已经很旧了，洗得都发白了。
   _____

   08) 阿姨送了我一双漂亮的银**筷**子作为生日礼物。
   _____

   09) 我每次回国都会给家人和朋友们带**礼**物。
   _____

   10) 我的行**李**不多，可以自己坐地铁去飞机场。
   _____

   11) 这个年轻人不但有**理**想而且还很有远见。
   _____

   12) 他能考上北京大学的**历**史系都是因为他自己的努**力**。
   _____

   13) 她有一双**蓝**色的眼睛，十分好看。
   _____

2. Translate the following sentences into Chinese.

01) I'm thirsty. Do you have any water?
_____

02) Grandma is not used to the air conditioner.
_____

03) China's population is the largest in the world.
_____

04) She was crying and laughing at the same time.
_____

05) Where did you get these blue trousers?
_____

06) Can you teach me how to use chopsticks?
_____

07) The gift was too expensive.
_____

08) She only took one piece of luggage for this travelling.
_____

09) He finally found his dream job.
_____

10) He is not clever but he is very hardworking.
_____

3. Listen, translate and repeat the recorded sentences.

01) 你口**渴**吗？要喝杯水吗？
_____

02) 那所房子**空**了几个月了。
_____

03) 听小**李**同学的口气，他时时**刻**刻都很努力。
_____

04) 他小时候老爱**哭**鼻子，一遇到事就**哭**。
_____

05）妹妹又长高了，**裤**子又短了。

06）这是我第一次用**筷**子吃饭。

07）这件用**蓝**纸包的**礼**物是送给你的。

08）小红说她的**理**想是成为一名一名好的**历**史老师。

# Lesson 34  485–496 脸、练、炼、辆、聊、料、邻、留、楼、绿、马、满

**All the exercises below are based on the combinations and phrases containing characters** 脸, 练, 炼, 辆, 聊, 料, 邻, 留, 楼, 绿, 马 and 满.

1. Translate the following sentences into English.

01) 刚刚跑完步，弟弟的**脸**蛋儿红得像个红苹果。
_____

02) 已经七点了，我们还要**练**吗？不**练**的话，我就回家了。
_____

03) 奶奶经常锻**炼**，所以虽然她已经九十多岁了，可身体还很好。
_____

04) 我家那**辆**旧自行车你拿去用吧。
_____

05) 放假了，天天在家和朋友打电话**聊**天儿，觉得没有意思了，这个周末我们去打球吧！
_____

06) 她一回家，**马**上开始**料**理家务事。
_____

07) 我们院子里住的都是近三十年的的老**邻**居了，每家人**都**十分友好。
_____

08) 下课后，你能**留**下来把你的地理笔记借我看一下吗？
_____

09) **楼**上的老张下个月就要搬到城东的新**楼**房去了。
_____

10) 我家那条街上新开张的小菜店里只卖**绿**色健康的菜。
_____

11) 小李怎么还没来？你们先走吧，我**留**下来再等一会儿吧。
_____

12) 我选的这间茶馆你还**满**意吗？他家的白茶很有名。
_____

练习 Lesson 34

2. Translate the following sentences into Chinese.

01) There are many tall buildings in the city.

02) Xiao Huang's neighbour has a big black cat.

03) What drink would you like?

04) The colour of this car is very nice.

05) Do you want to do some exercise right now?

06) I need to practise my handwriting.

07) You look pale, are you sick?

08) The school football coach is southerner.

09) What are you chatting about?

10) I saved a piece of cake for you.

3. Listen, translate and repeat the recorded sentences.

01) 妈妈最喜欢的颜色是绿色，不是蓝色。

02) 你不是要练习你的听力吗？电影马上就要开始了。

03) 我对你的回答很满意。

04) 小李九月去西班牙留学，他爸妈认为他去外国锻炼锻炼很好。

**05)** 楼下新开了一家茶馆儿,我们去那儿聊天好吗?

_____

**06)** 这是什么饮料?真好喝。

_____

**07)** 她高兴得满脸笑容。

_____

**08)** 这辆自行车是我的邻居的。

_____

# Lesson 35  497–508 冒、帽、末、目、拿、南、难、鸟、努、爬、怕、盘

**All the exercises below are based on the combinations and phrases containing characters** 冒, 帽, 末, 目, 拿, 南, 难, 鸟, 努, 爬, 怕 **and** 盘.

1. Translate the following sentences into English.

01) 上完一天的课以后回到家，看见饭桌上冒着热气的饭菜，我觉得饿得不得了。

02) 下火车时我把刚刚买的蓝帽子忘在了车上，等我想起来时车已经开走了，我怕再也找不回来了。

03) 下星期一是公共假日，所以这个周末我们有三天休息，真是太好了。

04) 这个数目是错的，你得重新算一次。

05) 别的饭菜我都不会做，只有做面条还算拿手。

06) 三、四月正是南方雨季的时候。

07) 你的脸色很难看，有什么地方不舒服吗？

08) 天上很多鸟往南边飞，一定是去南方过冬。

09) 你很聪明，只要好好努力，就一定能考上一所好大学。

10) 这是老楼，所以没有电梯，我们得爬六层楼梯上去。

11) 夏老师说这次数学考试题目难是难些，不过班上还是有一位同学得了满分。

12) 茶盘里的四个茶杯都是新买的。

2. Translate the following sentences into Chinese.

01) I am stuck on this question.

02) Let's work together to finish the program.

03) There are two birds sitting in the tree and singing!

04) The south is hotter than the north in the summer.

05) She goes swimming every weekend.

06) I like your hat. Where did you get it?

07) He only has two big plates and two small plates.

08) I'm not coming to work today because I have a cold.

09) I can't swim because I am afraid of water.

10) Please help me. I can't carry all the luggage by myself.

3. Listen, translate and repeat the recorded sentences.

01) 她是南方人。

02) 爸爸要去爬山看候鸟，所以到三月末才回北京。

03) 这种果树每年夏末才会结果。

04) 新年晚会的节目单已经公开了。

05）这个**难**题到现在还没解决。

06）他一直很**努**力，也不**怕**累。

07）水果**盘**里有苹果和香蕉。你吃吧，别客气！

08）雨下得很大，还很冷，要是没有雨伞和**帽**子，我不想**冒**雨出去。

# Lesson 36  509–520 胖、皮、啤、片、平、瓶、其、奇、骑、且、轻、清

**All the exercises below are based on the combinations and phrases containing characters** 胖, 皮, 啤, 片, 平, 瓶, 其, 奇, 骑, 且, 轻 **and** 清.

1. Translate the following sentences into English.

01) 他比我们去年见面时**胖**多了。

02) 这双新**皮**鞋才刚穿了一星期就坏了。

03) 叔叔喜欢一边儿看电视一边儿喝**啤**酒。

04) 这张照**片**是我们今年夏天在西班牙时照的。

05) 他**平**时不努力学习,所以一到考试心里就七上八下的。

06) 这**瓶**红酒是朋友特意从法国带回来送我的。

07) 大哥说我的马**骑**得不错,**其**实这是我第一次来马场学**骑**马。

08) 我很好**奇**她是怎么认识我哥哥的。

09) 她不但歌唱得好,而**且**舞也跳得很不一般。

10) 小红迟到了,所以她**轻轻**地走进了会议室。

11) 电视机的声音太大了,我听不**清**楚你在讲什么。

08) 我不会**骑**自行车,你能教我吗?

练习 Lesson 36

2. Translate the following sentences into Chinese.

01) The writing is too small to see clearly.

02) She looks very young.

03) This pair of leather shoes looks nice and is not expensive.

04) I don't drink beer, I drink red wine.

05) Where did you get all these photos?

06) Which restaurant do you usually go to for meals?

07) How much does this bottle of Coca Cola cost?

08) Do you have anything else to say?

09) His voice is very strange.

10) This is my first riding lesson.

3. Listen, translate and repeat the recorded sentences.

01) 哥哥的儿子很**胖**很白，而**且**很调**皮**。

02) 在所有的酒里，他最爱喝**啤**酒。

03) 这张是爷爷年**轻**时**骑**马的照**片**。

04) 一路平安，我们明年在北京见！

05）这个花瓶是我今天**清**早买的，你喜欢吗？
___

06）别看我没有猫和狗，**其**实我很喜欢小动物。
___

07）他**平**时穿着很**奇**特。
___

08）这个行李箱虽然看上去很大**其**实很轻。
___

# Lesson 37  521–532 秋、求、趣、裙、容、如、赛、伞、扫、山、衫、烧

**All the exercises below are based on the combinations and phrases containing characters** 秋, 求, 趣, 裙, 容, 如, 赛, 伞, 扫, 山, 衫 **and** 烧.

1. Translate the following sentences into English.

01) 一年四季中我最喜欢的季节是**秋**天。

02) 她想都没想就一口答应了小方的要**求**。

03) 这么多漂亮的**裙**子我都不知道该选哪一条了。

04) 小明对体育活动不感兴**趣**，他的兴**趣**都在电脑游戏上。

05) 我好不**容**易才买到周六音乐会的票，可你怎么又不想去了？

06) **如**果明天天气好我们就去爬**山**，好吗？

07) 这是他第五次参加比**赛**，也是他最后的一次比**赛**。

08) 外面在下雨呢，你带**伞**了吗？

09) 这个房间好久没人住了，需要好好打**扫**一下。

10) 这里**山**上的空气清新，是平时总是住在城市里的人休假的好地方。

11) 这件蓝衬**衫**是我新买的，你看好看吗？

12) 我感冒发**烧**了，已经两天没上班了。

2. Translate the following sentences into Chinese.

01）What are your requirements?

02）The colour of your skirt is very pretty.

03）What are you most interested in?

04）Today's maths test is easy.

05）Can we go to cinema tonight if you are free?

06）You are coming to the match, aren't you?

07）Is that your umbrella by the door?

08）We can go hiking this weekend.

09）These two shirts are new, and just in time for the autumn.

10）She has finished cleanning the room and is preparing for the dinner while waiting for her good friend.

3. Listen, translate and repeat the recorded sentences.

01）这条裙子和这件衬衫对你来说都太长了。

02）我特别喜欢看又大又亮的中秋月亮。

03）读书是她的兴趣爱好。

04）别担心，烧这一道菜很容易。

05）如果你不去山上，我也不去了。

06）今晚的比赛对他来说特别重要。

07）我的雨伞不见了，我求你了，借我一把伞好吗？

08）请你等一会儿，清扫工正在打扫房间呢。

# Lesson 38   533–544 声、实、史、世、市、瘦、叔、舒、束、树、数、刷

**All the exercises below are based on the combinations and phrases containing characters** 声, 实, 史, 世, 市, 瘦, 叔, 舒, 束, 树, 数 **and** 刷.

1. Translate the following sentences into English.

01) 房间里一点儿**声**音都没有，她可能睡着了。
_____

02) 我上周末**实**在是哪儿都没去，一直都在家看书。
_____

03) 他对历**史**很感兴趣，所以在大学学的是历**史**。
_____

04) 她用五年时间写的小说终于问**世**了。
_____

05) 这个城**市**的绿化很好，像个大花园。
_____

06) 这个月我哥哥一直在加班，人**瘦**了不少。
_____

07) 虽然**叔叔**和我爸爸不住在一个城市，可他们经常见面。
_____

08) 回家后干干净净地洗个澡，然后好好地睡一觉，第二天你就会觉得**舒**服了。
_____

09) 你怎么迟到这么久，球赛都快结**束**了。
_____

10) 小鸟在我家花园里的大**树**上安了家。
_____

11) 除了少**数**几个人以外，大多数人都如期完成了作业。
_____

12) 我在超市新买的那把牙**刷**，才用了没有多久就坏了。
_____

练习 Lesson 38

2. Translate the following sentences into Chinese.

01) It's really quiet in the classroom. There isn't a single sound.

02) I don't actually like beer. I prefer red wine.

03) He works in the university's History Department but not as a teacher.

04) That supermarket is big and clean.

05) That tall and slim girl is my friend.

06) My uncle is getting married this summer.

07) This chair is not comfortable to sit on.

08) She left before the film was over.

09) There are many newly planted trees along the pavement.

10) Remember to bring your own toothbrush.

3. Listen, translate and repeat the recorded sentences.

01) 大叔，电视机的声音太响了，你能开得轻一点儿吗？

02) 这是一个天天被刷新的真实的故事。

03) 聪聪的妈妈是一位很好的历史老师。过年了，应该送她一束鲜花。

04) 我的愿望是周游世界。

05）那个城**市**离我们这儿不远。
_____

06）她最近**瘦**了很多。
_____

07）新买的那张床睡着可真**舒**服。
_____

08）他是我们班的**数**学天才。
_____

# Lesson 39  545–556 双、算、特、疼、梯、提、甜、调、铁、头、突、图

**All the exercises below are based on the combinations and phrases containing characters** 双, 算, 特, 疼, 梯, 提, 甜, 调, 铁, 头, 突 and 图.

1. Translate the following sentences into English.

01) 我昨天出门脚上穿的两只鞋子不是一**双**的，**特**可笑。

02) 我**算**了**算**，长期租车的钱比坐出租车贵多了。

03) 这瓶香水是我**特**意从法国带回来给你的。

04) 你还**疼**吗？如果**疼**得实在不行的话，就吃药吧。

05) 办公室在三楼，我们是走楼**梯**还是坐电**梯**上去？

06) 对于你刚才**提**到的问题，我会在下周给你答复。

07) 你不吃饭只吃**甜**点是不可以的！

08) 这个夏天热得家里的空**调**需要二十四小时都开着。

09) 我哥哥和她哥哥的关系很**铁**。

10) 遇到的问题越多，**头**脑越要冷静。

11) 因为这场**突**如其来的大雪，所有的中小学都放了一天假。

12) 因为快考试了，学校的**图**书馆在晚自习的时间里都坐满了学生。

2. Translate the following sentences into Chinese.

01) This pair of trainers is for running.

02) He plans to go to Canada for the New Year.

03) He is an especially important guest to our hotel.

04) I have had headache for two days.

05) The lift has already been out of order for three days.

06) The bag you gave me is too heavy to lift.

07) She looked at me and gave me a sweet smile.

08) There is no air conditioning on the subway.

09) She is looking at a railway map of China.

10) He suddenly left the company and nobody knows why.

3. Listen, translate and repeat the recorded sentences.

01) 你的那**双**球鞋呢？

02) 明年夏天你打**算**去哪儿，你**提**前想过没有？

03) 她**疼**得脸都白了。

04) 能把你们家的**铁**梯子借我用一用吗？

05）这个西瓜又大又**甜**，**特**别好吃。

06）这几天**突**然变热了，商场里开足了空**调**。

07）站在最左边的那个人是我们的**头**儿。

08）下课后他总是在**图**书馆里，不是看书就是画**图**。

# Lesson 40  557–568 腿、碗、万、网、忘、位、文、闻、物、戏、夏、鲜

**All the exercises below are based on the combinations and phrases containing characters** 腿, 碗, 万, 网, 忘, 位, 文, 闻, 物, 戏, 夏 and 鲜.

1. Translate the following sentences into English.

01) 爷爷和奶奶今年一个九十二岁，一个九十三岁，**腿**脚都不太方便了。
_____

02) 你真能吃，两个小时以前才吃了一大**碗**面，怎么这么快就又饿了？
_____

03) 山上的天气和山下的不同，是千变**万**化的，一会儿晴天，一会儿下雨，一会儿又出大太阳了。
_____

04) 你上**网**查查，公司的**网**站上有这次活动的信息。
_____

05) 我今天早上出门**忘**记带手机了，没有它真不方便。
_____

06) 平常下午电影院里人很少，有很多空**位**子可以选。
_____

07) 他半年以前没了工作，现在已经是身无分**文**了。
_____

08) 等你回国后把你在西班牙的所见所**闻**都告诉我们吧。
_____

09) 她每次去山里都会给当地的小孩儿带很多礼**物**。
_____

10) 他近来天天玩儿游**戏**机，学习的心思都没了。
_____

11) 这个**夏**天你哪儿都不能去，得在家好好学习，准备秋天的考试。
_____

12) 新开张的超市里刚来了很多新**鲜**的水果，不过大多数是进口的。
_____

练习 Lesson 40

2. Translate the following sentences into Chinese.

01）My legs hurt after two hours of walking.

02）My mum bought the same bowl as yours.

03）Ten thousand tickets were sold out by nine o'clock this morning.

04）She bought this bicycle online.

05）I forgot that you work here.

06）Where is your seat?

07）I have smelt fragrance of the flowers, and you?

08）Do you know how to play this word game?

09）We will go to Xi'an in the summer and buy you a present then.

10）Today's fish is very fresh, incredibly fresh.

3. Listen, translate and repeat the recorded sentences.

01）你怎么老踢我的**腿**？

02）**夏**天，我做饭你洗**碗**，冬天再换回来怎么样？

03）爷爷不会上**网**也不会用电脑，**万**一有什么事怎么办？

04）我过了一个又新**鲜**又难**忘**的假期。

05) 对不起，戏票卖完了，你要的这个位子已经有人了。
_____

06) 钟先生对中国历史和文化很感兴趣。
_____

07) 我喜欢边吃饭边看新闻。
_____

08) 世界上有很多奇奇怪怪的动物。
_____

# Lesson 41  569–580 相、香、箱、响、向、像、鞋、心、信、熊、须、需

**All the exercises below are based on the combinations and phrases containing characters** 相,香,箱,响,向,像,鞋,心,信,熊,须 **and** 需.

1. Translate the following sentences into English.

01) 现在照**相**机卖得不好，因为大家一般都用手机上的照**相**机照**相**了。

02) 这瓶进口**香**水很贵，花了我两个月的零用钱。

03) 我自己一个人住，所以不需要大冰**箱**。

04) 不要在图书馆里大声说话，别影**响**到别人看书。

05) 我知道她是好**心**，可是常常好**心**办坏事。

06) 我都没有一件**像**样的裙子，下个月怎么去参加好朋友的婚礼啊。

07) 你已经试了好几双皮**鞋**了，现在决定买哪一双了吗？

08) 这么久都没接到姐姐的**信**了，我妈妈特别担**心**。

09) 张老师一**向**都相**信**自己教的学生的实力，认为他们在这次数学比赛中能得到好成绩。

10) 大**熊**猫长得实在可爱，所以大家都很喜爱它。

11) 每个人上飞机前都必**须**经过机场的安检。

12) 老人院里的不少老人腿脚都不行，上下楼梯的时候，**需**要别人的帮助。

2. Translate the following sentences into Chinese.

01) This is my camera. Where is yours?

02) Bananas are my favourite fruit.

03) This box is full of books, so it's very heavy.

04) The television is too loud.

05) She has no sense of direction.

06) My brother has two pairs of trainers that are never worn.

07) I believe that you will get into medical school.

08) It's late, I need to get going.

09) What she said and what she thought were not the same.

10) Nobody can satisfy his needs.

3. Listen, translate and repeat the recorded sentences.

01) 就这些钱，买了照相机就没有钱买鞋了。

02) 妈妈爱吃苹果，爸爸爱吃香蕉。

03) 冰箱里的牛奶过期了。

04) 你手机的声音太响了，需要把声音调小一点儿！

05）我表姐很喜欢开车，可是她的方向感很差。

06）我好像听到后面有熊的叫声。

07）他一不小心把门关上了，所以进不去了。

08）弟弟来信说，爸爸的病很重，必须马上送医院。

# Lesson 42  581–592 选、牙、阳、爷、业、姨、议、易、音、银、饮、应

**All the exercises below are based on the combinations and phrases containing characters** 选,牙,阳,爷,业,姨,议,易,音,银,饮 and 应.

1. Translate the following sentences into English.

01) 这两束花我都很喜欢，不知道该**选**哪一束送给老师。

02) **爷爷**如果没了他的假**牙**饭都吃不了，所以他很爱护他的假**牙**。

03) 今天我起床起得很晚，**阳**光已经照到我的床上了。

04) 我的邻居老大**爷**虽然已经快九十岁了，可是他身体还是很健康。

05) 今天我妹妹有很多作**业**，一吃完饭她就回房间做作**业**去了。

06) 她从小和她阿**姨**生活在一起，所以她们的感情很好。

07) 会**议**一结束他就急急忙忙地回家了。

08) 这道菜看起来很容**易**做，其实要做好它一点儿也不容**易**。

09) 他是本市**音**乐学院一年级的学生，他的老师是一位有名的**音**乐家。

10) 她离开学校后的十年一直在一家法国**银**行工作。

11) 商店里卖的**饮**料五花八门*，什么都有。

12) 他**应**该昨天晚上就回家了，可是因为一些事情没做完，所以今天早上才离开办公室。

练习　Lesson 42

2. Translate the following sentences into Chinese.

01) The location for the meeting has been selected.

02) He forgot to bring his toothbrush.

03) The summer's sun is like a big fire ball.

04) My grandad likes to watch football matches.

05) He just started his own business.

06) My auntie has been a dentist for 30 years.

07) She is easy to satisfy.

08) I have loved music since I was young.

09) The banks in this country are closed at the weekend.

10) My neighbour's favourite drink should be beer.

3. Listen, translate and repeat the recorded sentences.

01) 他**选**择了一家最便宜的酒店，附近有家中国**银**行。

02) 我明天会**议**以后应该到**牙**医那里去做检查。

03) 后天是我**爷爷**一百岁的生日，人的年岁能到一百，**应**该说很不容**易**啊！

04）这条商业街闻名世界。
_____

05）园园是我阿姨最小的女儿。
_____

06）他们一家都是音乐爱好者。
_____

07）这段日子太阳总是很好，没下雨。
_____

08）爸爸从超市买回来很多不同的饮料。
_____

# Lesson 43  593–604 迎、用、邮、又、于、育、遇、元、园、愿、越、澡

**All the exercises below are based on the combinations and phrases containing characters** 迎, 用, 邮, 又, 于, 育, 遇, 元, 园, 愿, 越 **and** 澡.

1. Translate the following sentences into English.

01) 为了**迎**接春节的到来，妈妈把家里的里里外外 * 打扫得干干净净 **。

02) 我把你给我的钱**用**来租了一辆跑车。

03) 我的电脑坏了，所以没法子查看我的电子**邮**件。

04) 市中心那家五星酒店的床**又**大**又**舒服。

05) 近两个月以来，她常常去找心理医生，出**于**对她的照顾，老板没有让她天天上班。

06) 在所有的体**育**比赛中，小高最愿意参加的是篮球比赛。

07) 看你一直不说话，是不是**遇**到了什么不开心的事？

08) 买这么一条小裙子要花三百加拿大**元**，别开玩笑了！

09) 每天早上爷爷和奶奶都去公**园**锻炼身体。

10) 我不在乎你**愿**意不**愿**意，我都要去学法文。

11) 近几个月她对我**越**来**越**不好，于是我们最终分了手。

12) 晚上睡觉前洗个热水**澡**该有多舒服啊！

2. Translate the following sentences into Chinese.

01) He is very welcome to visit our home.

02) She spends all her time writing short stories for the newspaper.

03) I asked him for two novelty stamps, each with a face value of five yuan.

04) The bananas in this store cost only five yuan per jin, so I bought three jin.

05) My younger brother doesn't like to play sports; he only likes to play computer games.

06) She met a musical genius at the evening party.

07) I really don't want to go to work over the weekend. I should go to the park instead.

08) I am enjoying my work more and more.

09) He looks as if he hasn't had a bath for a while.

10) The apples mum bought yesterday are big and red.

3. Listen, translate and repeat the recorded sentences.

01) 妈妈到门口去**迎**接客人了。

02) "元"是很常**用**的字词，不管愿意不愿意都必须记住。

03) 能留下你的电话和电子**邮**箱吗？

04）我爸爸是在中学教体育的老师。

05）上星期在北京的一条大街上，我遇见了老朋友李小明。

06）校园是不是干净、漂亮在于我们是不是常常打扫。

07）风越刮越大了，我们回不了家了。

08）他一边洗澡一边唱歌，非常快乐。

# Lesson 44  605–618  择、张、照、者、直、终、种、重、周、主、注、自、总、嘴

**All the exercises below are based on the combinations and phrases containing characters** 择，张，照，者，直，终，种，重，周，主，注，自，总 and 嘴.

1. Translate the following sentences into English.

01) 因为方便，所以越来越多的人选择在网上买东西。

02) 他很关注这张报纸上的新闻，所以他读了一次又一次。

03) 这张照片上的老人是她爸爸的爷爷。

04) 他嘴上说能自己照顾自己，实际上他做不到。

05) 她的小说在报纸上发表后不久就收到了很多读者的来信。

06) 李老师从早上开始就一直都在忙，直到下午三点才有空吃饭。

07) 我姐姐用了一天的时间终于把房间清扫干净了。

08) 我想了种种办法最终都没能解决这个难题，只能请教你了。

09) 这么重大的决定我自己作不了主，我得和大家商量一下。

10) 你能把周老师下周的西班牙语课表发到我的手机上吗？

11) 她相信自己一定能在这次游泳比赛中拿第一。

12) 他总是迟到，而且每次都有借口，大家已经习惯了。

练习 Lesson 44

2. Translate the following sentences into Chinese.

01) I have no choice but to wait for him to come back.

02) I will give you a piece of paper to write down your question.

03) This black and white photo is very old.

04) The author of this book is a seventeen-year-old girl.

05) After leaving the bank, he never found an ideal job.

06) I finally finished writing this book.

07) I have drunk many different types of coffee.

08) This suitcase is very heavy and I can't lift it at all.

09) The main seasoning ingredient for this dish is cola.

10) She has good grades and always comes the first.

3. Listen, translate and repeat the recorded sentences.

01) 他选择的这家饭馆离我住的宾馆很近。

02) 市中心的商场下个月开张。

03) 这几天我很忙，你能多照顾一下我妈妈吗？

04) 她们分别了二十几年，今天终于见面了。

05）我丈夫这几**周总**是加班，没有休息过。

_____

06）那**种**药是从法国进口的，中国现在还没有。

_____

07）这些是关于公司人事调动的文件，十分**重**要，不可以带出公司。

_____

08）夫妻双方天天在一起，**自**然会遇到问题，应该**注**意的是小事情**嘴**上让一让就没事了。**主**要的事情，慢慢地解决。

_____

练习答案
Key to exercises

# Lesson 1

1. 01) B  02) E  03) C  04) A  05) D  06) B
   07) D  08) A  09) C  10) B  11) E  12) E

2. 饱—bǎo   办—bàn   搬—bān   把—bǎ   矮—ǎi   板—bǎn
   半—bàn   啊—ā/á/ǎ/à   包—bāo   般—bān   安—ān   阿—ā/ē

3. 01) 1 / ˉ   02) 3 / ˇ   03) 3 / ˇ   04) 1 / ˉ   05) 4 / ˋ   06) 1 / ˉ
   07) 1 / ˉ ; 2 / ˊ ; 3 / ˇ ; 4 / ˋ   08) 1 / ˉ   09) 3 / ˇ   10) 3 / ˇ   11) 4 / ˋ   12) 1 / ˉ

4. 01) D  02) C  03) K  04) B  05) H / J  06) I
   07) F  08) E / L  09) J / H  10) G  11) L / E  12) A

5. 01) 搬 / 般  02) 矮  03) 把  04) 包  05) 啊  06) 安
   07) 般 / 搬  08) 饱  09) 阿  10) 板  11) 办 / 半  12) 半 / 办

6. 01) 般  02) 把  03) 搬  04) 安  05) 半  06) 包
   07) 板  08) 饱  09) 阿  10) 啊  11) 办  12) 矮

# Lesson 2

1. 01) C  02) E  03) A  04) B  05) C  06) E
   07) A  08) A  09) E  10) D  11) D  12) C

2. 必—bì   才—cái   层—céng   冰—bīng   参—cān   鼻—bí
   查—chá   差—chā/chà   变—biàn   被—bèi   尝—cháng   草—cǎo

3. 01) 4 / ˋ   02) 3 / ˇ   03) 2 / ˊ   04) 1 / ˉ   05) 2 / ˊ   06) 2 / ˊ
   07) 2 / ˊ   08) 1 / ˉ ; 4 / ˋ   09) 1 / ˉ   10) 4 / ˋ   11) 2 / ˊ   12) 4 / ˋ

4. 01) E  02) G  03) J  04) D  05) I  06) F
   07) B  08) C  09) K  10) A  11) L  12) H

5. 01) 鼻  02) 冰  03) 草  04) 才  05) 层  06) 被
   07) 变  08) 参  09) 必  10) 尝  11) 查  12) 差

6. 01) 差  02) 尝  03) 草  04) 查  05) 层  06) 参
   07) 必  08) 变  09) 被  10) 鼻  11) 才  12) 冰

# Lesson 3

1. 01) C  02) B  03) A  04) D  05) B  06) E  07) B
   08) D  09) B  10) A  11) D  12) A  13) D

2. 城—chéng  成—chéng  楚—chǔ  迟—chí  超—chāo  带—dài  聪—cōng
   衬—chèn  词—cí  除—chú  答—dā/dá  船—chuán  春—chūn

3. 01) 3 / ˇ  02) 4 / ˋ  03) 1 / ˉ  04) 2 / ˊ  05) 4 / ˋ  06) 2 / ˊ  07) 1 / ˉ
   08) 2 / ˊ  09) 2 / ˊ  10) 2 / ˊ  11) 1 / ˉ ; 2 / ˊ  12) 2 / ˊ  13) 1 / ˉ

4. 01) G/K  02) B  03) L  04) I  05) M  06) K/G  07) A
   08) E  09) F  10) D  11) H  12) J  13) C

5. 01) 成 / 城  02) 带  03) 超  04) 迟  05) 楚  06) 城 / 成  07) 春
   08) 船  09) 除  10) 答  11) 聪  12) 衬  13) 词

6. 01) 带  02) 聪  03) 成  04) 楚  05) 词  06) 城  07) 答
   08) 超  09) 衬  10) 迟  11) 船  12) 除  13) 春

# Lesson 4

1. 01) A  02) C  03) E  04) C  05) B  06) D
   07) A  08) D  09) B  10) A  11) D  12) D

2. 地—dì / de  担—dān/dàn  典—diǎn  当—dāng/dàng  单—dān  定—dìng
   锻—duàn  段—duàn  朵—duǒ  冬—dōng  短—duǎn  灯—dēng

3. 01) 1 / ˉ  02) 1 / ˉ ; 4 / ˋ  03) 4 / ˋ  04) 4 / ˋ ; 0 / ·  05) 3 / ˇ  06) 4 / ˋ
   07) 1 / ˉ ; 4 / ˋ  08) 3 / ˇ  09) 3 / ˇ  10) 1 / ˉ  11) 4 / ˋ  12) 1 / ˉ

4. 01) K  02) D  03) F  04) G / I  05) C  06) H
   07) L  08) E  09) J  10) I / G  11) B  12) A

5. 01) 朵  02) 段 / 锻  03) 冬  04) 段 / 锻  05) 定  06) 短
   07) 典  08) 灯  09) 地  10) 担  11) 当  12) 单

6. 01) 定  02) 典  03) 地  04) 灯  05) 当  06) 单
   07) 担  08) 冬  09) 朵  10) 短  11) 段  12) 锻

## Lesson 5

1. 01) B  02) D  03) A  04) A  05) D  06) A
   07) E  08) D  09) B  10) E  11) B  12) C

2. 发—fā/fà  该—gāi  耳—ěr  饿—è  法—fá/fǎ  风—fēng
   而—ér  复—fù  干—gān/gàn  方—fāng  附—fù  放—fàng

3. 01) 1 / ˉ  02) 4 / ˋ  03) 3 / ˇ  04) 1 / ˉ ; 4 / ˋ  05) 2 / ˊ ; 3 / ˇ  06) 1 / ˉ
   07) 4 / ˋ  08) 2 / ˊ  09) 4 / ˋ  10) 1 / ˉ  11) 1 / ˉ  12) 4 / ˋ

4. 01) H  02) K  03) J  04) D  05) F  06) L
   07) G  08) C  09) A  10) B / I  11) E  12) I / B

5. 01) 法  02) 饿  03) 耳  04) 干  05) 方  06) 复 / 附
   07) 放  08) 而  09) 该  10) 风  11) 发  12) 附 / 复

6. 01) 放  02) 该  03) 风  04) 法  05) 干  06) 发
   07) 饿  08) 方  09) 复  10) 耳  11) 附  12) 而

## Lesson 6

1. 01) B  02) E  03) C  04) A  05) D  06) B
   07) A  08) E  09) A  10) B  11) D  12) C

2. 刚—gāng  更—gēng/gèng  糕—gāo  感—gǎn  刮—guā  顾—gù
   根—gēn  害—hài  故—gù  惯—guàn  怪—guài  跟—gēn

3. 01) 1 / ˉ  02) 1 / ˉ ; 4 / ˋ  03) 4 / ˋ  04) 3 / ˇ  05) 1 / ˉ  06) 4 / ˋ
   07) 1 / ˉ  08) 4 / ˋ  09) 1 / ˉ  10) 4 / ˋ  11) 4 / ˋ  12) 1 / ˉ

4. 01) C / G  02) G / C  03) B  04) A  05) J  06) E / H
   07) F  08) I  09) D  10) H / E  11) L  12) K

5. 01) 更  02) 跟 / 根  03) 害  04) 糕  05) 感  06) 故 / 顾
   07) 怪  08) 刮  09) 根 / 跟  10) 顾 / 故  11) 刚  12) 惯

6. 01) 糕  02) 感  03) 刚  04) 跟  05) 惯  06) 顾
   07) 故  08) 根  09) 更  10) 刮  11) 怪  12) 害

## Lesson 7

1. 01) B    02) A    03) E    04) C    05) C    06) D
   07) A    08) E    09) A    10) B    11) A    12) D

2. 婚—hūn    坏—huài    河—hé    画—huà    黄—huáng    环—huán
   花—huā    乎—hū    行—háng/xíng    护—hù    化—huà    换—huàn

3. 01) 1 / ˉ    02) 4 / ˋ    03) 2 / ˊ    04) 1 / ˉ    05) 2 / ˊ    06) 2 / ˊ
   07) 4 / ˋ    08) 1 / ˉ    09) 2 / ˊ    10) 4 / ˋ    11) 4 / ˋ    12) 4 / ˋ

4. 01) H    02) F    03) L    04) E    05) D    06) J
   07) I    08) B    09) C / K    10) A    11) K / C    12) G

5. 01) 行    02) 花    03) 环    04) 乎    05) 婚    06) 护
   07) 换    08) 河    09) 化    10) 黄    11) 画    12) 坏

6. 01) 坏    02) 画    03) 乎    04) 化    05) 环    06) 行
   07) 换    08) 花    09) 护    10) 黄    11) 婚    12) 河

## Lesson 8

1. 01) B    02) C    03) E    04) C    05) B    06) D    07) E
   08) A    09) D    10) A    11) B    12) C    13) D    14) C

2. 记—jì    讲—jiǎng    加—jiā    或—huò    检—jiǎn    健—jiàn    简—jiǎn
   极—jí    季—jì    假—jià/jiǎ    急—jí    绩—jì    级—jí    己—jǐ

3. 01) 3 / ˇ    02) 3 / ˇ ; 4 / ˋ    03) 1 / ˉ    04) 4 / ˋ    05) 4 / ˋ    06) 4 / ˋ    07) 3 / ˇ
   08) 2 / ˊ    09) 4 / ˋ    10) 3 / ˇ    11) 2 / ˊ    12) 4 / ˋ    13) 2 / ˊ    14) 3 / ˇ

4. 01) F    02) B/K/L    03) H    04) L/B/K    05) D/J/M    06) K/L/B    07) A/E
   08) I    09) E/A    10) G    11) C    12) J/M/D    13) M/D/J    14) N

5. 01) 假    02) 记 / 季 / 绩    03) 绩 / 记 / 季    04) 或    05) 急 / 极 / 级
   06) 简 / 检    07) 级 / 急 / 极    08) 讲    09) 己    10) 加
   11) 健    12) 极 / 级 / 急    13) 检 / 简    14) 季 / 绩 / 记

6. 01) 讲    02) 健    03) 或    04) 极    05) 季    06) 级    07) 记

08) 加　　09) 绩　　10) 假　　11) 检　　12) 简　　13) 急　　14) 己

## Lesson 9

1. 01) C　02) E　03) E　04) D　05) A　06) B
   07) D　08) A　09) A　10) D　11) A　12) B

2. 结—jiē/jié　蕉—jiāo　解—jiě　借—jiè　角—jiǎo/jué　斤—jīn
   脚—jiǎo　接—jiē　街—jiē　节—jié　较—jiào　界—jiè

3. 01) 2 / ˊ ; 3 / ˇ　02) 4 / ˋ　03) 1 / ˉ　04) 1 / ˉ　05) 3 / ˇ　06) 1 / ˉ
   07) 4 / ˋ　08) 4 / ˋ　09) 1 / ˉ　10) 3 / ˇ　11) 2 / ˊ　12) 1 / ˉ ; 2 / ˊ

4. 01) K　02) F　03) G　04) C　05) L / B　06) D
   07) E　08) H / I　09) J　10) B / L　11) A　12) I / H

5. 01) 蕉　02) 角　03) 解　04) 斤　05) 结　06) 接 / 街
   07) 节　08) 界 / 借　09) 脚　10) 街 / 接　11) 较　12) 借 / 界

6. 01) 街　02) 解　03) 借　04) 结　05) 斤　06) 较
   07) 蕉　08) 脚　09) 界　10) 接　11) 角　12) 节

## Lesson 10

1. 01) A　02) C　03) D　04) C　05) C　06) D
   07) A　08) C　09) E　10) A　11) A　12) D

2. 句—jù　静—jìng　卡—kǎ/qiǎ　据—jù　决—jué　净—jìng
   酒—jiǔ　久—jiǔ　境—jìng　康—kāng　旧—jiù　居—jū

3. 01) 4 / ˋ　02) 1 / ˉ　03) 3 / ˇ　04) 3 / ˇ　05) 2 / ˊ　06) 4 / ˋ
   07) 3 / ˇ　08) 4 / ˋ　09) 4 / ˋ　10) 4 / ˋ　11) 4 / ˋ　12) 1 / ˉ

4. 01) I　02) F / J / K　03) C / L　04) E / H　05) H / E　06) B
   07) K / F / J　08) J / K / F　09) D　10) G　11) A　12) L / C

5. 01) 酒 / 久　02) 决　03) 据 / 句　04) 久 / 酒　05) 居　06) 康
   07) 净 / 静 / 境　08) 卡　09) 旧　10) 境 / 净 / 静　11) 静 / 境 / 净　12) 句 / 据

6. 01) 康　02) 境　03) 酒　04) 旧　05) 居　06) 句

07) 久　　08) 静　　09) 据　　10) 卡　　11) 决　　12) 净

# Lesson 11

1. 01) A　02) D　03) D　04) E　05) B　06) A　07) B
   08) A　09) C　10) E　11) E　12) A　13) B

2. 裤—kù　渴—kě　理—lǐ　空—kōng/kòng　历—lì　刻—kè
   口—kǒu　李—lǐ　礼—lǐ　力—lì　筷—kuài　哭—kū　蓝—lán

3. 01) 1/ˉ　02) 3/ˇ　03) 4/ˋ　04) 2/ˊ　05) 4/ˋ　06) 3/ˇ　07) 4/ˋ
   08) 3/ˇ　09) 3/ˇ　10) 3/ˇ　11) 4/ˋ　12) 4/ˋ　13) 1/ˉ; 4/ˋ

4. 01) G　02) H/I/K　03) C　04) A　05) I/K/H　06) F/L　07) E
   08) B　09) K/H/I　10) D　11) L/F　12) M　13) J

5. 01) 蓝　02) 裤　03) 渴　04) 筷　05) 李/礼/理　06) 力/历　07) 口
   08) 礼/理/李　09) 理/李/礼　10) 刻　11) 历/力　12) 哭　13) 空

6. 01) 哭　02) 渴　03) 理　04) 历　05) 蓝　06) 刻　07) 口
   08) 李　09) 筷　10) 裤　11) 礼　12) 力　13) 空

# Lesson 12

1. 01) E　02) A　03) C　04) D　05) E　06) D
   07) B　08) C　09) C　10) E　11) A　12) D

2. 炼—liàn　练—liàn　楼—lóu　脸—liǎn　邻—lín　料—liào
   马—mǎ　聊—liáo　满—mǎn　绿—lǜ　留—liú　辆—liàng

3. 01) 3/ˇ　02) 2/ˊ　03) 2/ˊ　04) 3/ˇ　05) 4/ˋ　06) 4/ˋ
   07) 4/ˋ　08) 4/ˋ　09) 3/ˇ　10) 2/ˊ　11) 2/ˊ　12) 4/ˋ

4. 01) D/H　02) L　03) A　04) K　05) G　06) F
   07) H/D　08) J　09) I　10) B　11) C　12) E

5. 01) 聊　02) 绿　03) 脸　04) 邻　05) 辆　06) 料
   07) 炼/练　08) 满　09) 楼　10) 留　11) 马　12) 练/炼

6. 01) 练　02) 马　03) 料　04) 聊　05) 绿　06) 楼

|  |  |  |  |  |  |
|---|---|---|---|---|---|
| 07) 辆 | 08) 满 | 09) 留 | 10) 脸 | 11) 炼 | 12) 邻 |

## Lesson 13

1. 01) A  02) D  03) B  04) B  05) C  06) A
   07) B  08) A  09) A  10) A  11) C  12) D

2. 帽—mào  爬—pá  盘—pán  努—nǔ  冒—mào  拿—ná
   目—mù  难—nán/nàn  怕—pà  末—mò  南—nán  鸟—niǎo

3. 01) 2 / ´  02) 2 / ´  03) 4 / `  04) 3 / ˇ  05) 2 / ´  06) 4 / `
   07) 4 / `  08) 2 / ´ ; 4 / `  09) 2 / ´  10) 4 / `  11) 4 / `  12) 3 / ˇ

4. 01) B  02) D / J  03) G  04) H  05) F  06) L
   07) J / D  08) K  09) E  10) C  11) I  12) A

5. 01) 冒 / 帽  02) 难  03) 目  04) 盘  05) 末  06) 拿
   07) 怕  08) 爬  09) 努  10) 南  11) 帽 / 冒  12) 鸟

6. 01) 南  02) 难  03) 帽  04) 目  05) 冒  06) 鸟
   07) 拿  08) 爬  09) 末  10) 努  11) 盘  12) 怕

## Lesson 14

1. 01) D  02) E  03) A  04) D  05) C  06) A
   07) A  08) B  09) C  10) B  11) E  12) C

2. 片—piàn/piān  胖—pàng  清—qīng  奇—qí  骑—qí  瓶—píng
   平—píng  啤—pí  皮—pí  其—qí  且—qiě  轻—qīng

3. 01) 4 / `  02) 2 / ´  03) 2 / ´  04) 2 / ´  05) 1 / ¯  06) 2 / ´
   07) 1 / ¯  08) 3 / ˇ  09) 2 / ´  10) 2 / ´  11) 1 / ¯ ; 4 / `  12) 2 / ´

4. 01) C / D  02) G / H  03) B / I / J  04) H / G  05) K  06) E
   07) D / C  08) A  09) I / J / B  10) J / B / I  11) F / L  12) L / F

5. 01) 皮 / 啤  02) 其 / 奇 / 骑  03) 胖  04) 片  05) 平 / 瓶  06) 骑 / 其 / 奇
   07) 奇 / 骑 / 其  08) 啤 / 皮  09) 瓶 / 平  10) 清 / 轻  11) 轻 / 清  12) 且

6. 01) 清  02) 平  03) 胖  04) 片  05) 皮  06) 啤

| | 07) 瓶 | 08) 其 | 09) 奇 | 10) 骑 | 11) 轻 | 12) 且 |

## Lesson 15

1. 
| 01) A | 02) B | 03) B | 04) C | 05) A | 06) C |
| 07) C | 08) E | 09) E | 10) A | 11) D | 12) A |

2. 
| 趣—qù | 求—qiú | 扫—sǎo | 秋—qiū | 容—róng | 山—shān |
| 赛—sài | 烧—shāo | 裙—qún | 如—rú | 衫—shān | 伞—sǎn |

3. 
| 01) 1 / ˉ | 02) 1 / ˉ | 03) 2 / ´ | 04) 2 / ´ | 05) 3 / ˇ | 06) 4 / ` |
| 07) 4 / ` | 08) 1 / ˉ | 09) 2 / ´ | 10) 2 / ´ | 11) 1 / ˉ | 12) 3 / ˇ |

4. 
| 01) J / K | 02) G | 03) L | 04) H | 05) B | 06) A |
| 07) E | 08) I | 09) D | 10) C | 11) K / J | 12) F |

5. 
| 01) 烧 | 02) 求 | 03) 如 | 04) 山 / 衫 | 05) 容 | 06) 扫 |
| 07) 秋 | 08) 趣 | 09) 裙 | 10) 伞 | 11) 衫 / 山 | 12) 赛 |

6. 
| 01) 衫 | 02) 扫 | 03) 求 | 04) 山 | 05) 如 | 06) 秋 |
| 07) 赛 | 08) 烧 | 09) 趣 | 10) 容 | 11) 裙 | 12) 伞 |

## Lesson 16

1. 
| 01) A | 02) D | 03) E | 04) A | 05) D | 06) B |
| 07) B | 08) C | 09) C | 10) B | 11) E | 12) B |

2. 
| 实—shí | 舒—shū | 刷—shuā | 瘦—shòu | 叔—shū | 声—shēng |
| 束—shù | 市—shì | 史—shǐ | 数—shǔ/shù | 树—shù | 世—shì |

3. 
| 01) 1 / ˉ | 02) 4 / ` | 03) 3 / ˇ ; 4 / ` | 04) 1 / ˉ | 05) 4 / ` | 06) 2 / ´ |
| 07) 1 / ˉ | 08) 1 / ˉ | 09) 3 / ˇ | 10) 4 / ` | 11) 4 / ` | 12) 4 / ` |

4. 
| 01) D / I | 02) F | 03) E | 04) K | 05) I / D | 06) C |
| 07) B / L | 08) L / B | 09) H | 10) J | 11) A / G | 12) G / A |

5. 
| 01) 史 | 02) 叔 / 舒 | 03) 刷 | 04) 数 | 05) 世 / 市 | 06) 声 |
| 07) 束 / 树 | 08) 市 / 世 | 09) 树 / 束 | 10) 实 | 11) 舒 / 叔 | 12) 瘦 |

6. 
| 01) 叔 | 02) 数 | 03) 史 | 04) 树 | 05) 舒 | 06) 实 |

07) 世　　08) 市　　09) 束　　10) 瘦　　11) 声　　12) 刷

## Lesson 17

1. 01) B　02) C　03) A　04) D　05) C　06) A
   07) B　08) E　09) B　10) A　11) B　12) B

2. 调—diào/tiáo　算—suàn　双—shuāng　提—tí　图—tú　头—tóu
   疼—téng　铁—tiě　梯—tī　特—tè　甜—tián　突—tū

3. 01) 2 / ´　02) 2 / ´　03) 4 / `　04) 1 / ¯　05) 3 / ˇ　06) 1 / ¯
   07) 1 / ¯　08) 2 / ´ ; 4 / `　09) 2 / ´　10) 4 / `　11) 2 / ´　12) 2 / ´

4. 01) A　02) J　03) B　04) F　05) D　06) C
   07) K　08) I　09) E　10) L　11) G　12) H

5. 01) 调　02) 梯　03) 特　04) 算　05) 图　06) 双
   07) 突　08) 提　09) 甜　10) 铁　11) 头　12) 疼

6. 01) 提　02) 特　03) 突　04) 调　05) 双　06) 算
   07) 图　08) 梯　09) 甜　10) 头　11) 铁　12) 疼

## Lesson 18

1. 01) A　02) C　03) A　04) D　05) B　06) C
   07) E　08) D　09) A　10) B　11) E　12) B

2. 夏—xià　腿—tuǐ　文—wén　鲜—xiān　碗—wǎn　闻—wén
   忘—wàng　物—wù　万—wàn　戏—xì　网—wǎng　位—wèi

3. 01) 3 / ˇ　02) 3 / ˇ　03) 4 / `　04) 2 / ´　05) 3 / ˇ　06) 4 / `
   07) 4 / `　08) 4 / `　09) 4 / `　10) 1 / ¯　11) 4 / `　12) 2 / ´

4. 01) C　02) A　03) I　04) E / K　05) G　06) H
   07) B　08) D　09) J　10) L　11) K / E　12) F

5. 01) 网　02) 碗　03) 万　04) 文 / 闻　05) 夏　06) 位
   07) 闻 / 文　08) 物　09) 鲜　10) 戏　11) 腿　12) 忘

6. 01) 网　02) 万　03) 腿　04) 闻　05) 忘　06) 物

| | 07) 夏 | 08) 戏 | 09) 文 | 10) 碗 | 11) 鲜 | 12) 位 |

## Lesson 19

1. 
| | 01) D | 02) B | 03) E | 04) B | 05) A | 06) B |
|---|---|---|---|---|---|---|
| | 07) A | 08) E | 09) D | 10) B | 11) C | 12) A |

2. 须—xū  心—xīn  响—xiǎng  向—xiàng  相—xiāng/xiàng  熊—xióng
   鞋—xié  箱—xiāng  需—xū  香—xiāng  像—xiàng  信—xìn

3. 
| | 01) 1 / ˉ | 02) 1 / ˉ | 03) 2 / ´ | 04) 1 / ˉ | 05) 1 / ˉ | 06) 1 / ˉ |
|---|---|---|---|---|---|---|
| | 07) 4 / ` | 08) 1 / ˉ ; 4 / ` | 09) 2 / ´ | 10) 3 / ˇ | 11) 4 / ` | 12) 4 / ` |

4. 
| | 01) C | 02) A / I | 03) K | 04) F | 05) D / J | 06) L |
|---|---|---|---|---|---|---|
| | 07) E | 08) G / H | 09) B | 10) I / A | 11) J / D | 12) H / G |

5. 
| | 01) 信 | 02) 相 | 03) 响 | 04) 心 | 05) 熊 | 06) 像 / 向 |
|---|---|---|---|---|---|---|
| | 07) 鞋 | 08) 香 / 箱 | 09) 需 / 须 | 10) 箱 / 香 | 11) 向 / 像 | 12) 须 / 需 |

6. 
| | 01) 熊 | 02) 需 | 03) 须 | 04) 心 | 05) 信 | 06) 香 |
|---|---|---|---|---|---|---|
| | 07) 相 | 08) 鞋 | 09) 向 | 10) 响 | 11) 箱 | 12) 像 |

## Lesson 20

1. 
| | 01) D | 02) A | 03) E | 04) C | 05) B | 06) A |
|---|---|---|---|---|---|---|
| | 07) D | 08) E | 09) B | 10) A | 11) C | 12) C |

2. 银—yín  饮—yǐn  音—yīn  阳—yáng  业—yè  选—xuǎn
   姨—yí  爷—yé  牙—yá  易—yì  应—yīng/yìng  议—yì

3. 
| | 01) 3 / ˇ | 02) 2 / ´ | 03) 2 / ´ | 04) 2 / ´ | 05) 2 / ´ | 06) 1 / ˉ |
|---|---|---|---|---|---|---|
| | 07) 3 / ˇ | 08) 4 / ` | 09) 4 / ` | 10) 1 / ˉ ; 4 / ` | 11) 2 / ´ | 12) 4 / ` |

4. 
| | 01) G | 02) K | 03) I | 04) L | 05) B | 06) E |
|---|---|---|---|---|---|---|
| | 07) F | 08) C / J | 09) A | 10) J / C | 11) H | 12) D |

5. 
| | 01) 银 | 02) 议 / 易 | 03) 爷 | 04) 音 | 05) 牙 | 06) 选 |
|---|---|---|---|---|---|---|
| | 07) 阳 | 08) 业 | 09) 饮 | 10) 易 / 议 | 11) 姨 | 12) 应 |

6. 
| | 01) 牙 | 02) 饮 | 03) 选 | 04) 音 | 05) 业 | 06) 易 |
|---|---|---|---|---|---|---|

07) 银 08) 议 09) 爷 10) 应 11) 姨 12) 应

## Lesson 21

1. 01) B 02) E 03) A 04) D 05) D 06) A
   07) A 08) E 09) A 10) B 11) D 12) B

2. 澡—zǎo 又—yòu 元—yuán 用—yòng 愿—yuàn 越—yuè
   邮—yóu 遇—yù 育—yù 园—yuán 于—yú 迎—yíng

3. 01) 4 / ˋ 02) 3 / ˇ 03) 2 / ˊ 04) 4 / ˋ 05) 4 / ˋ 06) 4 / ˋ
   07) 4 / ˋ 08) 2 / ˊ 09) 2 / ˊ 10) 2 / ˊ 11) 2 / ˊ 12) 4 / ˋ

4. 01) D / J 02) K 03) E / H 04) I 05) B 06) G
   07) F 08) C 09) A 10) J / D 11) H / E 12) L

5. 01) 元 / 园 02) 又 03) 遇 / 育 04) 邮 05) 愿 06) 迎
   07) 澡 08) 于 09) 越 10) 园 / 元 11) 育 / 遇 12) 用

6. 01) 邮 02) 遇 03) 迎 04) 又 05) 育 06) 元
   07) 愿 08) 园 09) 于 10) 越 11) 澡 12) 用

## Lesson 22

1. 01) A 02) A 03) D 04) D 05) B 06) B 07) E
   08) D 09) C 10) D 11) B 12) A 13) A 14) B

2. 自—zì 周—zhōu 注—zhù 择—zé 种—zhǒng / zhòng 直—zhí
   重—zhòng / chóng 终—zhōng 张—zhāng 者—zhě 照—zhào
   主—zhǔ 嘴—zuǐ 总—zǒng

3. 01) 3 / ˇ 02) 2 / ˊ 03) 4 / ˋ 04) 3 / ˇ 05) 1 / ˉ 06) 3 / ˇ ; 4 / ˋ
   07) 2 / ˊ 08) 1 / ˉ 09) 4 / ˋ 10) 4 / ˋ 11) 1 / ˉ 12) 4 / ˋ ; 2 / ˊ
   13) 3 / ˇ 14) 3 / ˇ

4. 01) C 02) K 03) F 04) D 05) L 06) G 07) E
   08) A 09) I 10) H 11) B 12) J 13) N 14) M

5. 01) 种 02) 张 03) 照 04) 择 05) 自 06) 直 07) 重

| | 08) 者 | 09) 终 | 10) 周 | 11) 主 | 12) 注 | 13) 嘴 | 14) 总 |

6. 01) 照　　02) 张　　03) 种　　04) 择　　05) 主　　06) 重　　07) 注
   08) 者　　09) 直　　10) 终　　11) 自　　12) 周　　13) 总　　14) 嘴

# Lesson 23　　349-360

1. 我**阿姨**明天**飞**北京。
2. 他很刻**板**。
3. 这是谁的书**包**啊？
4. 她很**矮**，所以总是穿高跟鞋。
5. 老师**把**名单写在了黑**板**上。
6. 这桌子太重了，我一个人**搬**不动。
7. 大家都在图书馆里**安**静地看着书。
8. 我会找到解决问题的**办**法。
9. 我吃了两个**包**子了，已经**饱**了。
10. 这蛋糕我们一人一**半**好吗？

# Lesson 24　　361-372

1. 我们都**被**他的故事感动了。
2. 我的**鼻**子很疼。
3. 明天早上八点你**必**须到那儿。
4. 你知道火车时刻表有了新的**变**化吗？
5. 这个**冰**箱太大了，搬不进那个房间。
6. 我刚**才**去过那个超市了。
7. 你想**参**加这次比赛吗？
8. 我很高兴这个决定是公司高**层**做（出）的。
9. 这个检票员正在检**查**每个人的票。
10. 你想**尝**试一下这种新鲜的绿茶吗？

# Lesson 25　　373-385

1. 你平时是在**超**市买东西吗？
2. 我刚买了两件**衬**衫，一件是绿色的，还有一件是蓝色的。
3. 我们能准时完**成**这个工作。
4. 这个**城**市有大学吗？
5. 他**迟**早会来的。
6. **除**了他自己，没人能帮他。
7. 我还是不清**楚**你想要什么。

8. 开**春**以后／**春**回大地他们住回了**船**上。

9. 你的**词**典在哪儿？

10. 他清楚地回**答**了老板提出的问题。

## Lesson 26    386-397

1. 能给我菜**单**吗？
2. 我**担**心你来不了了。
3. 我的花园里有五颜六色的花**朵**。
4. 你**当**然可以用我的字**典**。
5. 她快乐**地**唱着歌。
6. 我决**定**今天下午去游泳。
7. 你喜欢**冬**季运动吗？
8. 你的裙子太**短**了。
9. 他每个星期去健身房**锻**炼两次。
10. 他房间的**灯**一晚上都亮着。

## Lesson 27    398-408

1. 晚饭吃什么？我**饿**极了。
2. 这道菜不但看起来不错**而**且很好吃。
3. 你看没看见我的白色**耳**机？
4. 我用了很多种**方**法也查不出你的电脑有什么问题。
5. 我不相信她会那么**干**。
6. 今天**风**很大。
7. 你**放**心我会照顾好你的猫。
8. **附**近有咖啡店吗？
9. 你能再重**复**一次吗？
10. 你对工作应**该**更认真点儿。

## Lesson 28    410-421

1. 你有**感**冒药吗？
2. 他**刚**才还在这儿。我不知道他现在在哪儿。
3. 这蛋**糕**是谁做的？
4. **根**据电视新闻上说，明天**刮**大风。
5. 我晚上开车总是会**更**加小心。
6. 我去年在报纸上看到过这个**故**事。
7. 今天早上一个**顾**客都没有。
8. 在北方，春天经常**刮**风。

9. 他没来，我很奇**怪**。
10. 她不习**惯**晚上喝啤酒。

## Lesson 29    422-433

1. 你的**行**李怎么这么重？
2. 我们几**乎**不敢／能相信自己的眼睛。
3. 她找不着她的**护**照了。
4. 周日**花**市里有卖各种各样／五颜六色的**花**。
5. 我们知道市场已经有了变**化**。
6. 这是一张手**画**的草图。
7. 她终于找到了一个理想的**环**境。
8. 我的车**坏**了，所以现在只能**换**成坐公共汽车了。
9. 他对中国文**化**很感兴趣。
10. 这是一个快乐的**婚**礼。

## Lesson 30    434-447

1. 你可以穿晚礼服**或**者裙子去参加晚会。
2. 他非常担心自己的考试成**绩**。
3. 她看到她的礼物时高兴**极**了。
4. 我考试前着**急**得不得了，怕／担心这次过不了这一**级**。
5. 她可能忘**记**告诉他了。
6. 请给我一张**季**票好吗？
7. 上星期六只有五十个客人来参**加**米米的婚礼。
8. 经理给员工们放了一天**假**。
9. 你最好去做一次身体检**查**。
10. 他进步这么大，真不**简**单。

## Lesson 31    448-459

1. 我喜欢香**蕉**，也喜欢苹果。你呢？
2. 她是这出戏的主**角**。／在这出戏里，她是主**角**。
3. 我听到外面有**脚**步声。
4. 她比**较**喜欢长跑，不喜欢跳高。
5. 这个苹果给你，**接**着！
6. 过**街**时要注意车辆。
7. 比赛**结**果出来了。
8. 你（正）在看什么电视**节**目呢？
9. 这个难题还没得到**解**决，还需要时间。

10. 这个世界上是有很多新奇的东西的。

## Lesson 32　460-471

1. 楼梯打扫干净了吗？
2. 你能安静点吗？
3. 为了接/见经理，他在那儿站了很久。
4. 皮特不习惯喝很多酒，他觉得会对健康不好。
5. 她把那个旧铁箱当桌子用。
6. 我的邻居是个牙医。
7. 她觉得这句话十分风趣。
8. 他的害怕是有根据的。
9. 她终于下决心决定跟她丈夫离婚了。
10. 这家店不能刷卡。

## Lesson 33　472-484

1. 我渴了，你有水吗？
2. 奶奶不习惯用空调。
3. 中国的人口（是）世界第一。
4. 她一边哭一边笑。
5. 这条蓝裤子你是在哪儿买的？
6. 你能教我怎么用筷子吗？
7. 这礼物太贵重了。
8. 这次旅行她只带了一个行李箱。
9. 他终于/总算找到了他理想的工作。
10. 他虽然不聪明但是工作很努力。

## Lesson 34　485-496

1. 城里有很多高楼。
2. 小黄的邻居有一只大黑猫。
3. 你想喝什么饮料？
4. 这辆车的颜色真漂亮。
5. 你想现在马上去锻炼吗？
6. 我得/需要练习写字。
7. 你脸色（看起来）很白，是不是病了？
8. 这所学校的足球教练是个南方人。
9. 你们在聊什么呢？
10. 我留了一块蛋糕给你。

## Lesson 35    497-508

1. 我被这道题**难**住了。
2. 让我们一起来完成这个节**目**。
3. 树上坐着的两只**鸟**在唱歌呢!
4. **南**方的夏天比北方热。
5. 她每个周**末**去游泳。
6. 我喜欢你的**帽**子,你是在哪儿买的?
7. 他只有两个大**盘**子和两个小**盘**子。
8. 我感**冒**了所以今天不能来上班了。
9. 我不会游泳因为我**怕**水。
10. 你来帮帮我,我自己一个人**拿**不了这么多行李。

## Lesson 36    509-520

1. 这字太小了看不**清**楚。
2. 她看上去很年**轻**。
3. 这双**皮**鞋很好看,而**且**还不贵。
4. 我不喝**啤**酒,我喝红酒。
5. 你是在哪儿拿到这些照**片**的?
6. 你们**平**时去哪个饭馆儿吃饭?
7. 这**瓶**可乐多少钱?
8. 你还有什么**其**他要说的吗?
9. 他的声音很**奇**怪。
10. 这是我第一次上**骑**马课。

## Lesson 37    521-532

1. 你的要**求**是什么?
2. 你这条**裙**子的颜色很漂亮。
3. 你最感兴**趣**的是什么?
4. 今天的数学考试很**容**易。
5. **如**果今晚你有空,我们去看电影好吗?
6. 你会来看这场比**赛**的,是吧?
7. 门口那把**伞**是你的吗?
8. 这个周末我们可以去爬**山**。
9. 这两件衬**衫**是新的,正好**秋**天就能穿了。
10. 她已经打**扫**完房间、正准备**烧**水做饭,等着好朋友来呢。

## Lesson 38    533-544

1. 教室里真安静，一点儿**声**音都没有。
2. 其**实**我不喜欢喝啤酒，我喜欢喝红酒。
3. 他在大学历**史**系工作，但不是老师。
4. 那家超**市**又大又干净。
5. 那个又高又**瘦**的女孩子是我朋友。
6. 我**叔叔**今年夏天就要结婚了。
7. 这把椅子坐着／上去不**舒**服。
8. 电影还没结**束**她就离开了。
9. 人行道上新种了很多**树**。
10. 记得带上你自己的牙**刷**。

## Lesson 39    545-556

1. 这**双**运动鞋是跑步时穿的。
2. 他打**算**新年时去加拿大。
3. 他是我们酒店**特**别重要的一位贵宾／贵客。
4. 我**头疼**了两天了。
5. 这个电**梯**已经坏了三天了。
6. 你给我的这个包太重了，**我提**不动。
7. 她看着我，**甜甜**地笑了。
8. 地铁里没有空**调**。
9. 她在看一张中国**铁**路地**图**。
10. 他**突**然离开了公司，没人知道为什么。

## Lesson 40    557-568

1. 走路走了两个小时，我的双**腿**都疼了。
2. 我妈妈买的**碗**和你的（那个）一样。
3. 今天早上九点（的时候），一**万**张（门）票就都卖完了。
4. 这辆自行车是她在**网**上买的。
5. 我**忘**了你在这儿上班。
6. 你的**位**子在哪儿？
7. 我**闻**到了花香，你呢？
8. 你知道怎么玩儿这个**文**字游**戏**吗？
9. 今年**夏**天我们会去西安，到时候给你买礼**物**。
10. 今天的鱼很新**鲜**／**鲜**得不得了。

## Lesson 41    569-580

1. 这是我的照**相**机，你的在哪儿？
2. **香**蕉是我喜爱的水果。
3. 这**箱**子里都是书，很重。
4. 电视机的声音太**响**了。
5. 她一点儿方**向**感都没有。
6. 我弟弟有两双运动**鞋**，（还）从来没穿过。
7. 我相**信**你能考上医学院。
8. 很晚了，我必**须**得走了。
9. 她说的和她**心**里想的不一样。
10. 没人能满足他的**需**要。

## Lesson 42    581-592

1. 会**议**的地点已经**选**定了。
2. 他忘记带他的**牙**刷了。
3. 夏天的太**阳**像个大火球。
4. 我**爷爷**的爱好是看足球赛。
5. 他自己的事**业**才刚刚起步。
6. 我阿**姨**当**牙**医当了三十年了。
7. 她是很容**易**满足的。
8. 我从小就喜爱**音**乐。
9. 这个国家的**银**行周末都关门。
10. 我邻居最爱喝的**饮**料**应**该是啤酒。

## Lesson 43    593-604

1. 非常欢**迎**他来我们家。
2. 她的时间都**用**在给报纸写短文上了。
3. 我向他要了两张五**元**的新奇的**邮**票。
4. 这家的香蕉才卖五**元**一斤，**于**是我就买了三斤。
5. 我弟弟不喜欢体**育**运动，他只喜欢打游戏。
6. 晚会上她**遇**到了一位音乐天才。
7. 我实在不**愿**意周末去上班，周末应该去公**园**玩儿。
8. 我**越**来**越**喜欢我的工作了。
9. 他看上去好像很久没洗**澡**了。
10. 妈妈昨天买的苹果**又**大**又**红。

# Lesson 44    605-618

1. 我没的选**择**，只能等他回来。
2. 我给你一**张**纸，你把问题写下来。
3. 这张黑白**照**片很旧了。
4. 这本书的作**者**是一个17岁的女孩。
5. 离开银行后，他一**直**没有找到理想的工作。
6. 这本书我**终**于写完了。
7. 我喝过很多**种**不同的咖啡。
8. 这个行李箱非常**重**，我一点儿都提不起来。
9. 这道菜的**主**要调料是可乐。
10. 她成绩很好，**总**是拿第一。

**阅读篇**

# 路在我们的脚下

（第三部）（6500字小说）

## Reading for Lessons 23–44

# 前情摘要

钟天明、谢小星和高亮三个人是大学同学，先后到了英国伦敦来读书。钟天明的爸爸是书商，谢小星的爸爸是医生，高亮的爸爸妈妈都是老师。钟天明到英国以后，见到了自己在中国就很喜欢的一个女学生欢欢（白书欢），而且希望以后欢欢能跟他一起回国，帮助他在中国开几家像英国那样的书店。谢小星除了上学以外，同时还在一个小店里工作。在那里，她结识了一位叫班司的英国青年。而高亮在一所学校做汉语课的助手——这个课的主教老师叫常苹，也是从北京来伦敦的。

这一天，高亮要和以上说的几个朋友会面了。见面前，他告诉大家，他会带他的女朋友来参加他们这个伦敦的"五人帮"，这五个人是钟天明、谢小星、白书欢、常苹，还有他自己。

## Notes

1. Some characters are in square and bold : these are measure words.
2. Some characters are **in bold**: these are the grammatical codes.
3. Some characters are highlighted in grey with dotted key words: these are useful sentence patterns or phrases.
4. Some characters are underlined: these are proper nouns.
5. Some characters are marked with a curved line under them: these are idioms or set phrases.

# 路在我们的脚下（第三部）（31—52单篇注释版）

## 31

　　谁都没有想到的是①高亮这次是真的有女朋友了。刚听说这件事的时候，除了谢小星以外，大家都②想着这个人一定会是常苹。在几个人对这件"突发事件"的短信里③，只有谢小星的看法不同，她说，高亮的样子是很叫人喜欢的④，加上他又那么爱读书，一定会有一些女孩子看上他，所以一点儿也不奇怪。关于是不是常苹，她说，常苹是不会喜欢高亮这种人的，据她对常苹的了解⑤，高亮不是她选择的对象。关于谁会对常苹的路⑥，谢小星不愿意说。当别人问到高亮的女友会是英国人还是中国人的时候⑦，谢小星说，她觉得多半是英国人，还说，很可能是他们大学的同事。

　　这回"五人帮"中的四个人和以往不一样，大家都在着急地等着下一次的会面。当然，他们希望变成"六人帮"，也就是说⑧，加上这个高亮的女朋友。

## Grammatical Notes

① 谁都没有想到的是：no one expected that...

② 除了……以外，都……：except/apart from..., all others...

③ 在……里：in

④ 是……的：the sentence pattern emphasizing what goes in between the two words

⑤ 据 A 对 B：according to A of B....

⑥ 关于谁会对常苹的路：regarding who will match Chang Ping

⑦ 当……的时候：when

⑧ 就是说：in other words; that is to say

## 32

果然，会面那天高亮带来了一位高高瘦瘦、留着咖啡色长发的年轻女子。让大家感到新奇的是①，说她是中国人吧，可她的脸色红红白白，而且黑眼睛里带着一点儿绿，说她是英国人吧，可是②她的鼻子小小的，而且非常的周正。还有，她那大嘴一笑起来③，两个嘴角向上提，样子甜甜的。一句话④，这个女子从上到下、从头到脚都让人觉得又自然、又自在⑤、又舒服；再有一个意外中的意外⑥，就是她居然⑦还会说一口很不错的北京话！

### Grammatical Notes

① 让大家感到新奇的是：to everyone's surprise

② 说 A 是 B 吧，可是……，说 A 是 C 吧，可是……：if we say A is B, but..., if we say A is C, but....

③ 一笑起来：once [somebody] starts smiling

④ 一句话：in a word

⑤ 自在：self-confidence; a feeling of trust in one's abilities, qualities, and judgment

⑥ 意外中的意外：even more surprisingly

⑦ 居然：unbelievably

## 33

　　还没有等高亮向大家介绍，这位女子就①大大方方②地跟大家说："我叫简，你们一定读过那本英文小说《简·爱》，我的名字跟书中的女主人公③一样④，是Jane，变成北京话的发音，就很接近'简单'的'简'。我姓'顾'，'顾客'的'顾'。我爷爷是北京人，奶奶是法国人，所以我妈妈一半是法国人，一半是北京人。不过，我妈妈从小就⑤在英国读书，工作以后结识了我爸爸。我爸爸是地地道道⑥的英国伦敦人，所以我生在英国，不过我跟我妈妈姓⑦，姓顾。从小妈妈就⑧跟我说汉语，所以我的口语没有太大的问题，但是读和写很差。"

　　几个人听到顾简这么一说⑨，就都明白她为什么长得这么动人了。于是大家就你一句我一句地向她问起话来⑩。

### Grammatical Notes

① 还没有……就 : have not... yet, then...
② 大大方方 : carry oneself with ease and confidence
③ 女主人公 : female protagonist
④ 跟……一样 : the same as
⑤ 从小就…… : since childhood...
⑥ 地地道道 : one hundred percent; out-and-out
⑦ 跟……姓 : take the surname of
⑧ 从小妈妈就…… : since childhood, Mother...
⑨ 这么一说 : no one has expected that...
⑩ 问起话来 : start asking

## 34

　　<u>高亮</u>很有意思①，他坐在<u>顾简</u>的边上，一│句│话也②不说，只是看着她，听到有意思③的地方④就得体⑤**地**笑笑。<u>谢小星</u>轻轻**地**对着他的耳朵说："<u>高亮</u>，看**把**你得意⑥的。怎么，还急不急着回<u>北京</u>了？"

　　<u>高亮</u>小声**地**说："当然回，要是<u>简</u>也愿意，我就写信给学校，请她去<u>中国</u>做<u>英文</u>老师。<u>小星</u>，我听说你也有男朋友了，而且也是<u>英国人</u>，是吗？为什么不一起来？还非得我们请不可⑦吗？"

　　"没，还早呢，只是工作在一起而已⑧，再说一│个│星期只有上班的那一│天│能见着。不过，他很特别。"

　　"怎么特别？"<u>高亮</u>问。

　　<u>谢小星</u>说："说不上⑨。不过你放心，我是不会轻易有这│种│关系的。而且我爸爸特别的'<u>中国</u>'，他多半儿不喜欢我有一│个│非<u>中国人</u>⑩的男朋友。"

---

### Grammatical Notes

① 有意思：funny

② 也：at all

③ 有意思：interesting

④ 地方：parts (of the story); place

⑤ 得体：suitable; in appropriate terms

⑥ 得意：be proud of

⑦ 非得（děi）……不可：must. The double negatives of 非……不可 adding in here is even stronger than using 得 alone.

⑧ 而已：nothing more; that is all.

⑨ 说不上：It is difficult to say

⑩ 非中国人：foreign

## 35

"其实没关系，下次见面把他带来，也让我们见识见识①。"高亮说。谢小星越是这样说，高亮就越是②好奇。

那边几个人，特别是常苹对顾简就别提多热情了③。后来，她还主动要求，在下次去钟天明家的时候，她给大家做饭。

一直都不大说话的欢欢最后说："还是我来做饭吧，我做的菜，我爸爸妈妈都说比街上的饭馆都好。不过，我有一个先决④条件。"

钟天明马上⑤接过话说："什么先决条件？快说！"

谢小星笑笑，说："欢欢，我告诉你，钟天明对你提出的所有条件都会满足，你就是⑥要天上的月亮，他都能给你！"

钟天明说："对，就是别要太阳，怕是⑦我还没走到一半，就被烧化⑧了。"

### Grammatical Notes

① 见识见识 : widen one's knowledge; gain experience
② 越（是）……越（是）…… : the more...the more
③ 别提多……了 : exceptionally
④ 先决 : prerequisite; precondition
⑤ 马上 : immediately
⑥ 就是 : even
⑦ 怕是 : perhaps; afraid of
⑧ 烧化 : burn to melt

## 36

"其实条件很简单,你们五个人每人带一样礼物给我。"欢欢说。

"啊!你要的太多也太贵了吧!"常苹说。

"大家先听听欢欢要的都是什么样的礼物好不好?欢欢,你说说,你要求我们每人送你一件什么样的东西?"顾简说。

欢欢说:"还是顾简理解我。好,我的要求是你们送我一样最简单的、得是你们自己做的、决不可以是从外边买的,或者是别人给你们的东西。"

钟天明自作聪明①地加了一句:"一定得②是和做饭有关系的,对不对?"

欢欢说:"不对,得是和做饭没有关系的礼物。"

## Grammatical Notes

① 自作聪明: think oneself smart

② 得(děi): need to; have to

# 37

从上次见面到下次再会面的这三个星期里，钟天明一直睡不好觉①。去年夏天他回过国——那次欢欢没有回去，她的借口是大学第一年，她的英文虽然不错，但还是感到有点儿吃力②，所以她要用放假的两个多月参加一个英语班。钟天明明明知道是借口，也没有办法，只好一放假就③自己一个人回去了。今年，为了④实现他的新想法，他事先跟爸爸商议过，把他爸爸和妈妈都接来英国。妈妈当然是来看看儿子的生活环境，但是他爸爸主要是来参看⑤英国的同行⑥是怎么开书店的⑦。经过一个半月的调查 (diàochá, research)，同时也是在钟天明的说动下⑧，他爸爸下定了决心，准备参照英国书店的样子在中国的几个城市再开几家书店。前几天，他爸爸来电话说，已经从银行借到了第一笔钱，书店的地点也选择好了，是想在北京东城的一条商业街试开第一家。

## Grammatical Notes

① 睡不好觉：couldn't sleep well

② 吃力：hard; difficult

③ 一……就……：as soon as...

④ 为了：in order to; due to

⑤ 参看：see for reference

⑥ 同行（háng）：of the same trade or occupation

⑦ 是……的：pattern for emphasis

⑧ 在……下：inspired by...

## 38

"你最好在今年八月的时候回国，而且我希望头一两年，你出头做主①，当经理，我从后面帮助你。"钟天明的爸爸说。

这自然是一个好事情。当他把这件事告诉六人帮的时候，大家也都为他高兴②。

可是钟天明像一年前一样，他最想知道的是这次欢欢是怎么打算的③。他很清楚，她还在大学第二年春季的学期，如果她能答应他的请求，回北京给他的书店帮一点儿忙，也就是说，欢欢八月跟他一同回去的话，到九月中大学一开学，她马上就④可以回英国上学；他觉得要是能做到这样就太理想⑤了。所以这些天钟天明一直都在等欢欢的短信，可是左等右等，等了很久都等不来。钟天明真的不能想象这次又是自己一个人只身⑥回国而身边没有欢欢……

### Grammatical Notes

① 出头做主：be in charge
② 为他高兴：happy for him
③ 是……的：pattern for emphasis
④ 一……就……：as soon as...
⑤ 理想：ideal
⑥ 只身：alone; by oneself

## 39

　　白书欢知道钟天明要回国的信息以后很不平静。这个人身上的两样东西：男子汉气①和乐意帮助他人，早在就在她的心里生了根。但是她对他也有一些不满意的地方，比如：爱说大话，言过其实②，做事不认真，自以为是③。她不是没有想过三年学业完成以后，要不要跟他走得更近。不过，她总是有一种说不清道不明④的感觉：跟他走到一起以后，今生今世⑤就再不分离了吗？其实，这句话是⑥钟天明在上次会面后开车送她回学校的路上说的⑥。那天，钟天明一边⑦开车一边⑦唱歌，可是他把本来的歌词变成了"我会跟你在一起，今生今世不分离"。欢欢懂得他的用心，只是她还是像以往一样，眼睛不看着钟天明，而是望着汽车的前方。她已经感觉到自己的脸上是热热的，为了⑧不让钟天明看见，所以就把头向左边看。但是她知道，钟天明已经看出了她的心思。

## Grammatical Notes

① 男子汉气：manly

② 言过其实：overstate; exaggerate

③ 自以为是：consider oneself (always) in the right

④ 说不清道不明：be unable to explain clearly

⑤ 今生今世：all one's life

⑥ 是……的：pattern for emphasis

⑦ 一边……一边……：simultaneously; doing two things at the same time

⑧ 为了：in order to

## 40

　　事实上，这次六人帮在钟天明住的地方吃饭，白书欢主动要求自己来做饭，而且提出要其他的五个人一人送给她一件礼物，主要的意图是想考考钟天明：看一看他会送什么样的礼物给自己。她认为，看一个人是真心或是假意，是真对你好，还是假对你好，从三个星期后送她的礼物上就可以得知几分；当然，自己在①钟天明的心目中②是怎样的一种人，也是能从他选择什么样的东西给自己看出来的③。欢欢对自己的这个主意相当满意。换句话说，她是在等得到钟天明的礼物以后，才④会给他一个是不是跟他一起回国的答复。

　　三个星期后的那天是一个不冷不热的太阳天，大家分别带上自己的礼物来到了钟天明居住的房子。这些礼物分别是：两张打满了汉字的《英国游记》，一个手工刻出来的马头，一个真的蛋糕，一张伦敦公园春季的风景画和一只蓝色中带点儿绿色的纸做的鸟。

### Grammatical Notes

① 于：at
② 心目中：in the heart
③ 是……的：pattern for emphasis
④ 才：until

## 41

这 次 见面的时候，一开始大家就给白书欢出了 个 难题，要她说出这五 样 礼物分别都是出自谁的手笔①或手工。

"好，给我两分钟。"欢欢说，然后她 把 这几 样 礼物都看了又看，最后说："这 个 蛋糕是顾简做的。"

顾简说："对，是我做的，不过你是怎么知道的呢？"

"因为这是英国人从小学就必须学会的，是吧？"欢欢说。顾简点点头。然后，欢欢拿起《英国游记》，说："这一看就知道是高亮的文风。高亮，对不对？"

高亮说："这怪②我，其实我应该事先想到这一层。对，是我写的。你说对了。"

欢欢看了看那 张 画，说："这一定是谢小星的画，因为里面一共有四 条 狗和两 只 猫。"

## Grammatical Notes

① 手笔：one's handwriting
② 怪我：blame me

## 42

谢小星说:"没错,画着画着①我就**把**狗和猫画进去了。"

礼物里还有就是那**只**蓝中带绿的纸做的鸟和那**个**手工刻的马头了。

"当然,这**只**蓝绿色的鸟一定是常苹做的,因为我知道她在英国的学校教汉语,常常得用自己做的一**些**动物的手工来②帮助学生记住汉字。"

常苹说:"啊,真没想到,你平时不怎么爱说话,可真是**个**有心人啊,有**些**事、有**些**话我平时就是说说而已,可是你都记在心里头了。对对对,这**只**蓝绿色的鸟是我的大作。"

最后的一**个**马头,不用欢欢再说了,当然就是钟天明的手笔了。欢欢说:"钟天明平常最自以为是,所以他**把**自己比作马中的头儿,马头,其实就是'头马'③,换一**个**个儿④而已,就是说,能做出超常的成就来。天明,我说的对吧?"

## Grammatical Notes

① 画着画着 : during painting

② 用……来…… : use A for B

③ 头马 : head horse

④ 换一个个儿 : reverse the order

## 43

钟天明的脸一下子①就红了，急忙说："马是我刻的，可是没有你说的那层用意；只不过一时兴起②，就把它刻出来了。"

常苹半板着脸、半带着笑说："天明的礼物，两个成语就说清楚了。你们知道是哪两个吗？"

高亮急忙说："大家都别说，试试简的中文。"

顾简想用手机查，可是高亮一下子拿了过去，"不能从字典里找，你自己想，应该不太难。"

"啊，我想起来一个，是'一马当先'。"顾简一边叫一边说。

"对！"常苹说，"那么还有一个呢？"

顾简又想了想，然后老老实实③地说："我实在想不出来了，高亮你帮帮我。"

欢欢说："让天明自己说，他没准儿还说不上来呢！半分钟，超过就不算！自己给自己的东西命名，还不容易？"

### Grammatical Notes

① 一下子：suddenly
② 一时兴起：be a whim
③ 老老实实：honestly

## 44

"天马行空。"①钟天明没等欢欢把话说完，就把这个成语说出来了。

大家都说好，只有欢欢笑了笑，说："我想着你是要说'骑着马找马'②呢！"这么一说，除了钟天明一时没明白、顾简从来没听说过这个习语以外，其他几个人都知道欢欢的用意，就都会心③地笑了起来。

不过钟天明很快就明白欢欢说的是什么了。因为平时欢欢就话里有话④地说过他喜欢自以为是，也太自爱。而"天马行空"正是他最不应该用来回答的成语。但是他知道，话已经说出了口，就没有办法了。

## Grammatical Notes

① 天马行空：a heavenly steed soaring across the skies—a powerful and unconstrained style
② 骑着马找马：sit on one horse and look for another—hold onto one job while seeking another
③ 会心：understanding; knowing
④ 话里有话：the words imply more

# 45

那天,欢欢做的饭菜十分简单,几乎①就是英国人的饭菜:每样菜都是新鲜的,加上她还特地一大早②跑到很远的鱼市买来了鲜鱼。她还像英国人一样,把碗、筷子和上菜的盘子都洗得干净得发亮③。正好,钟天明家里有法国红酒,所以虽然菜不多,可是颜色十分好看,红是红,白是白,绿是绿,黄是黄。

看到这些,几个人都说,欢欢不再是大家眼里的"小小姐"了,而是一位"超女④"!

常苹说:"这些饭菜,还有碗筷盘子的明净,加上这些颜色,让我想起我们中间的一个人⑤。"

谢小星说:"我知道你的意思,是不是……"

## Grammatical Notes

① 几乎:almost
② 一大早:in the early morning
③ 洗得干净得发亮:wash very cleanly to the point of shining
④ 超女:super girl
⑤ 我们中间的一个人:one of us

## 46

　　常苹突然觉得自己的话头可能不大得体，就想打住①，不过这时顾简已经接过话来了，"我明白，常老师说的是我，对吗？"

　　虽然顾简说对了，可是常苹还是觉得很不好意思，就一口气连着说了好几个"对不起"，"对不起，对不起！我这个话说得有一点儿过火②了。"

　　"没关系，我不在乎③，我的同学和朋友们也常常开这样的玩笑，我已经习惯了。中国有句习语，叫'习惯成自然④'，对不对？！"

　　常苹接过话头⑤说："对啊！简，我真的觉得你很了不起，把汉语说得那么地道！我来英国以前，已经学了差不多十年的英语，在中国还教英语，现在我到伦敦也有两年多了，可是我的英语常常还是'京歌力师'⑤！"

　　大家听到"京歌力师"都笑得不行。

### Grammatical Notes

① 打住：stop
② 过火：go too far
③ 不在乎：do not care
④ 习惯成自然：habit becomes second nature
⑤ 京歌力师：pidgin for English

## 47

　　终于，白书欢在一次发手机短信的时候，同意了钟天明的请求，跟他一道回北京。

　　北京的八月和七月差不多，从早到晚①都很热。欢欢除了在自己家里以外②，常常去帮助钟天明准备开书店的事。钟天明有了这样一个可爱的小朋友在身边，自然是一天到晚都非常开心。不过，他有一件心事，每当想起来，都不舒服。这件事就是，欢欢很愿意跟他在一起，而且干起工作来③，一点儿都不怕累。但是，每次钟天明的爸爸妈妈来的时候，她不但不怎么说话，而且还常常找借口跑到别的地方去，一直到钟天明的爸爸妈妈离开了书店才④回来。钟天明虽然感到有些奇怪，可是他不想、也觉得不应该问，因为他知道，他和欢欢的关系还没有到可以告诉家里人的那一步。这层道理他懂，但在感情上，他还是有点儿过不去⑤。

### Grammatical Notes

① 从……到…… : from...to.... This pattern is not only used for time, but also for places, etc.
② 除了……以外 : except for/apart from...
③ 干起工作来 : after starting to work
④ 不但不……而且……一直……才…… : not only...but also...until...then...
⑤ 过不去 : cannot overcome; cannot get through

## 48

一个雨天，钟天明在没有得到欢欢的同意下，想给她一个意外：主动①开车去她的家接她。到了门口，他才发了一条信息。果然，五分钟以后，欢欢出来了。但是没有他想象的那么高兴。钟天明突然脑子一热，想进去看看欢欢的家，也向她的爸爸妈妈问一声好②。所以在欢欢从家里出来要上车的时候，他问："欢欢，我可以进去跟你的爸爸妈妈问一个好吗？"

没想到的是，欢欢非但一下子冷下了脸，而且③用比她的表情④更冰冷的语气回答说："钟天明同学！"这是欢欢与钟天明认识以来头一回这样叫他，"第一，你没经过我的同意就来我家，这本来就已经不太好了；第二，现在你又提出要进到我的家去看看，借口说想问候我的爸爸妈妈，你是不是太过分了⑤。天明，我看还是不必⑥了吧，你还是回去吧⑦。"

### Grammatical Notes

① 主动：actively

② 问一声好：say hello

③ 非但……而且……：not only but also...; the pattern is the same as 不但……而且……

④ 表情：facial expression

⑤ 太过分了：go too far

⑥ 不必：no need

⑦ 还是回去吧：would be better to go back; should go back

## 49

"为什么？我们是好朋友，而且我们都在<u>英国</u>留学，我只是想去看看他们，没有别的意思，来看看好朋友的爸爸妈妈，怎么就不行呢？"<u>钟天明</u>有点儿不高兴了，他觉得<u>欢欢</u>是在故意为难①他。

万没有料到的是②，<u>欢欢</u>一听这话<u>就</u>③更生气了，她二话没说④就跑回了家，还**把**门重重**地**关上了。

雨越下越大⑤，<u>钟天明</u>的脑子变成了空白，他发现自己都不会思考⑥了。其后，他就像那**个**自己刻出的马头一样，一动不动、没有知觉。很长时间以后，他才意识到外面的雨声已经没有了，而在光光的街上，他的汽车发动机⑦一直都在响着……

### Grammatical Notes

① 故意为难：intend to distress somebody
② 万没有料到的是：what I didn't expect is
③ 一……就……：as soon as...; once...then
④ 二话没说：didn't say anything
⑤ 越……越……：the more...the more...
⑥ 思考：think deeply; ponder over
⑦ 发动机：engine

## 50

　　以后的日子①对②钟天明来说就不同了：自那天起，白书欢就没有再去过书店。钟天明也没有再给她打电话或者发短信。思来想去③，他觉得一定是欢欢的家里发生过什么事情。可是会是什么事情呢？他不知道。慢慢的，这件事就变成了他心里一个解不开的结④，结果是他饭也吃不香，觉也睡不好。很快，他的妈妈先发现了这个问题，不过她明白，儿子的事她是问不出来的。于是她把自己的感觉告诉了丈夫。一天，那是在新书店要开始迎接顾客的前一个星期，钟天明突然对他爸爸说："欢欢不会来我们书店帮忙了。"

### Grammatical Notes

① 日子：life; time
② 对：to
③ 思来想去：think over
④ 结：knot

## 51

"是吗？她回英国了吗？"

"没有，只是她不会再来了。"

"出什么问题了？看样子，她不来对你影响不小，你妈妈早就发现你最近的心情很不正常了。告诉我，你们发生了什么事？"钟天明的爸爸问。

"我也不清楚。"于是，钟天明把那天去接欢欢的前前后后①一五一十②地说给了爸爸，他希望爸爸能帮助他想想，是不是欢欢的家里有过什么事。

"这个不难，要是你需要，我可以去打听③一下。不过，真的有必要吗？天明，欢欢跟你目前是什么关系？"

"这……这很难说。"

"你不说我们也看得出来，最少你对她是有感情的。其实欢欢来了没两天，我们就看出来了。你妈妈在第一次见到她的时候，就附在④我的耳朵上说'这个女孩子不简单'。"钟天明的爸爸说。

## Grammatical Notes

① 前前后后 : the details
② 一五一十 : the whole story
③ 打听 : ask about
④ 附在 : close to

## 52

"对,你们说得对。我很喜欢她,而且想跟她走得更近,希望她以后能成为我的女朋友。但是,她近**些**天的所作所为①,实在让我很担心。要是她这么不懂事,不顾别人的感觉,今后我们怎么在一起呢?"

"天明,先不要急着怪她②,你也应该做一做调查。我认为很有可能是她的家有过什么事,所以她不想要你进她的家,更不想让你见她的亲人。对了,你妈妈还说过,我们每**次**去书店的时候,她的样子都不很自然,而且十**次**有九**次**都借故③跑开,不和我们在一起。"

"这**个**我早就知道,可是跟你们一样,我也不清楚是为什么。"钟天明说。"虽然我们在英国来往得很多,差不多一两**个**星期就见一**次**面,平时也发发短信,可是我从来没有问过她家里是做什么的。我只知道她住的地方是**个**高干楼④,因为楼已经很旧了,我想里边住的那**些**人可能都是过去的高干,不是现在的。其他的我就都不了解了。您怎么调查呢?我也上网试过,可是因为我不知道她爸爸的名字和单位,所以什么都没有查到。"

"这样吧,我们都留意⑤一**些**,我也帮助你问问。"

……

## Grammatical Notes

① 所作所为 : one's behaviour or conduct
② 怪她 : blame her
③ 借故 : find an excuse
④ 高干楼 : the building specially built for high-ranking officials
⑤ 留意 : pay attention

# 路在我们的脚下（第三部）(31—52完整版)

## 31

谁都没有想到的是高亮这次是真的有女朋友了。刚听说这件事的时候，除了谢小星以外，大家都想着这个人一定会是常苹。在几个人对这件"突发事件"的短信里，只有谢小星的看法不同，她说，高亮的样子是很叫人喜欢的，加上他又那么爱读书，一定会有一些女孩子看上他，所以一点儿也不奇怪。关于是不是常苹，她说，常苹是不会喜欢高亮这种人的，据她对常苹的了解，高亮不是她选择的对象。关于谁会对常苹的路，谢小星不愿意说。当别人问到高亮的女友会是英国人还是中国人的时候，谢小星说，她觉得多半是英国人，还说，很可能是他们大学的同事。

这回"五人帮"中的四个人和以往不一样，大家都在着急地等着下一次的会面。当然，他们希望变成"六人帮"，也就是说，加上这个高亮的女朋友。

## 32

果然，会面那天高亮带来了一位高高瘦瘦、留着咖啡色长发的年轻女子。让大家感到新奇的是，说她是中国人吧，可她的脸色红红白白，而且黑眼睛里带着一点儿绿，说她是英国人吧，可是她的鼻子小小的，而且非常的周正。还有，她那大嘴一笑起来，两个嘴角向上提，样子甜甜的。一句话，这个女子从上到下、从头到脚都让人觉得又自然、又自在、又舒服；再有一个意外中的意外，就是，她居然还会说一口很不错的北京话！

## 33

还没有等高亮向大家介绍，这位女子就大大方方地跟大家说："我叫简，你们一定读过那本英文小说《简·爱》，我的名字跟书中的女主人公一样，是Jane，变成北京话的发音，就很接近'简单'的'简'。我姓'顾'，'顾客'的'顾'。我爷爷是北京人，奶奶是法国人，所以我妈妈一半是法国人，一半是北京人。不过，我妈妈从小就在英国读书，工作以后结识了我爸爸。我爸爸是地地道道的英国伦敦人，所以我生在英国，不过我跟我妈妈姓，姓顾。从小妈妈就跟我说汉语，所以我的口语没有太大的问题，但是读和写很差。"

几个人听到顾简这么一说，就都明白她为什么长得这么动人了。于是大家就你一句我一句地向她问起话来。

## 34

高亮很有意思，他坐在顾简的边上，一句话也不说，只是看着她，听到有意思的地方就得体地笑笑。谢小星轻轻地对着他的耳朵说："高亮，看把你得意的。怎么，还急不急着回北京了？"

高亮小声地说："当然回，要是简也愿意，我就写信给学校，请她去中国做英文老师。小星，我听说你也有男朋友了，而且也是英国人，是吗？为什么不一起来？还非得我们请不可吗？"

"没，还早呢，只是工作在一起而已，再说一个星期只有上班的那一天能见着。不过，他很特别。"

"怎么特别？"高亮问。

谢小星说："说不上。不过你放心，我是不会轻易有这种关系的。而且我爸爸特别的'中国'，他多半儿不喜欢我有一个非中国人的男朋友。"

## 35

"其实没关系，下次见面把他带来，也让我们见识见识。"高亮说。谢小星越是这样说，高亮就越是好奇。

那边几个人，特别是常苹对顾简就别提多热情了。后来，她还主动要求，在下次去钟天明家的时候，她给大家做饭。

一直都不大说话的欢欢最后说："还是我来做饭吧，我做的菜，我爸爸妈妈都说比街上的饭馆都好。不过，我有一个先决条件。"

钟天明马上接过话说："什么先决条件？快说！"

谢小星笑笑，说："欢欢，我告诉你，钟天明对你提出的所有条件都会满足，你就是要天上的月亮，他都能给你！"

钟天明说："对，就是别要太阳，怕是我还没走到一半，就被烧化了。"

## 36

"其实条件很简单，你们五个人每人带一样礼物给我。"欢欢说。

"啊！你要的太多也太贵了吧！"常苹说。

"大家先听听欢欢要的都是什么样的礼物好不好？欢欢，你说说，你要求我们每人送你一件什么样的东西？"顾简说。

欢欢说："还是顾简理解我。好，我的要求是你们送我一样最简单的、得是你们自己做的、决不可以是从外边买的，或者是别人给你们的东西。"

钟天明自作聪明地加了一句："一定得是和做饭有关系的，对不对？"

欢欢说："不对，得是和做饭没有关系的礼物。"

## 37

从上次见面到下次再会面的这三个星期里，钟天明一直睡不好觉。去年夏天他回过国——那次欢欢没有回去，她的借口是大学第一年，她的英文虽然不错，但还是感到有点儿吃力，所以她要用放假的两个多月参加一个英语班。钟天明明明知道是借口，也没有办法，只好一放假就自己一个人回去了。今年，为了实现他的新想法，他事先跟爸爸商议过，把他爸爸和妈妈都接来英国。妈妈当然是来看看儿子的生活环境，但是他爸爸主要是来参看英国的同行是怎么开书店的。经过一个半月的调查，同时也是在钟天明的说动下，他爸爸下定了决心，准备参照英国书店的样子在中国的几个城市再开几家书店。前几天，他爸爸来电话说，已经从银行借到了第一笔钱，书店的地点也选择好了，是想在北京东城的一条商业街试开第一家。

## 38

"你最好在今年八月的时候回国，而且我希望头一两年，你出头做主，当经理，我从后面帮助你。"钟天明的爸爸说。

这自然是一个好事情。当他把这件事告诉六人帮的时候，大家也都为他高兴。

可是钟天明像一年前一样，他最想知道的是这次欢欢是怎么打算的。他很清楚，她还在大学第二年春季的学期，如果她能答应他的请求，回北京给他的书店帮一点儿忙，也就是说，欢欢八月跟他一同回去的话，到九月中大学一开学的时候，她马上就可以回英国上学；他觉得要是能做到这样就太理想了。所以这些天钟天明一直都在等欢欢的短信，可是左等右等，等了很久都等不来。钟天明真的不能想象这次又是自己一个人只身回国而身边没有欢欢……

## 39

白书欢知道钟天明要回国的信息以后很不平静。这个人身上的两样东西：男子汉气和乐意帮助他人，早在就在她的心里生了根。但是她对他也有一些不满意的地方，比如：爱说大话，言过其实，做事不认真，自以为是。她不是没有想过三年学业完成以后，要不要跟他走得更近。不过，她总是有一种说不清道不明的感觉：跟他走到一起以后，今生今世就再不分离了吗？其实，这句话是钟天明在上次会面后开车送她回学校的路上说的。那天，钟天明一边开车一边唱歌，可是他把本来的歌词变成了"我会跟你在一起，今生今世不分离"。欢欢懂得他的用心，只是她还是像以往一样，眼睛不看着钟天明，而是望着汽车的前方。她已经感觉到自己的脸上是热热的，为了不让钟天明看见，所以就把头向左边看。但是她知道，钟天明已经看出了她的心思。

## 40

事实上，这次六人帮在钟天明住的地方吃饭，白书欢主动要求自己来做饭，而且提出要其他的五个人一人送给她一件礼物，主要的意图是想考考钟天明：看一看他会送什么样的礼物给自己。她认为，看一个人是真心或是假意，是真对你好，还是假对你好，从三个星期后送她的礼物上就可以得知几分；当然，自己在钟天明的心目中是怎样的一种人，也是能从他选择什么样的东西给自己看出来的。欢欢对自己的这个主意相当满意。换句话说，她是在等得到钟天明的礼物以后，才会给他一个是不是跟他一起回国的答复。

三个星期后的那天是一个不冷不热的太阳天，大家分别带上自己的礼物来到了钟天明居住的房子。这些礼物分别是：两张打满了汉字的《英国游记》，一个手工刻出来的马头，一个真的蛋糕，一张伦敦公园春季的风景画和一只蓝色中带点儿绿的纸做的鸟。

## 41

这次见面的时候,一开始大家就给白书欢出了个难题,要她说出这五样礼物分别都是出自谁的手笔或手工。

"好,给我两分钟。"欢欢说,然后她把这几样礼物都看了又看,最后说:"这个蛋糕是顾简做的。"

顾简说:"对,是我做的,不过你是怎么知道的呢?"

"因为这是英国人从小学就必须学会的,是吧?"欢欢说。顾简点点头。然后,欢欢拿起《英国游记》,说:"这一看就知道是高亮的文风。高亮,对不对?"

高亮说:"这怪我,其实我应该事先想到这一层。对,是我写的。你说对了。"

欢欢看了看那张画,说:"这一定是谢小星的画,因为里面一共有四条狗和两只猫。"

## 42

谢小星说:"没错,画着画着我就把狗和猫画进去了。"

礼物里还有就是那只蓝中带绿的纸做的鸟和那个手工刻的马头了。

"当然,这只蓝绿色的鸟一定是常苹做的,因为我知道她在英国的学校教汉语,常常得用自己做的一些动物的手工来帮助学生记住汉字。"

常苹说:"啊,真没想到,你平时不怎么爱说话,可真是个有心人啊,有些事、有些话我平时就是说说而已,可是你都记在心里头了。对对对,这只蓝绿色的鸟是我的大作。"

最后的一个马头,不用欢欢再说了,当然就是钟天明的手笔了。欢欢说:"钟天明平常最自以为是,所以他把自己比作马中的头儿,马头,其实就是'头马',换一个个儿而已,就是说,能做出超常的成就来。天明,我说的对吧?"

## 43

钟天明的脸一下子就红了,急忙说:"马是我刻的,可是没有你说的那层用意;只不过一时兴起,就把它刻出来了。"

常苹半板着脸、半带着笑说:"天明的礼物,两个成语就说清楚了。你们知道是哪两个吗?"

高亮急忙说:"大家都别说,试试简的中文。"

顾简想用手机查,可是高亮一下子拿了过去,"不能从字典里找,你自己想,应该不太难。"

"啊,我想起来一个,是'一马当先'。"顾简一边叫一边说。

"对!"常苹说,"那么还有一个呢?"

顾简又想了想,然后老老实实地说:"我实在想不出来了,高亮你帮帮我。"

欢欢说:"让天明自己说,他没准儿还说不上来呢!半分钟,超过就不算!自己给自己的东西命名,还不容易?"

## 44

"天马行空。"钟天明没等欢欢把话说完,就把这个成语说出来了。

大家都说好,只有欢欢笑了笑,说:"我想着你是要说'骑着马找马'呢!"这么一说,除了钟天明一时没明白、顾简从来没听说过这个习语以外,其他几个人都知道欢欢的用意,就都会心地笑了起来。

不过钟天明很快就明白欢欢说的是什么了。因为平时欢欢就话里有话地说过他喜欢自以为是,也太自爱。而"天马行空"正是他最不应该用来回答的成语。但是他知道,话已经说出了口,就没有办法了。

## 45

那天,欢欢做的饭菜十分简单,几乎就是英国人的饭菜:每样菜都是新鲜的,加上她还特地一大早跑到很远的鱼市买来了鲜鱼。她还像英国人一样,把碗、筷子和上菜的盘子都洗得干净得发亮。正好,钟天明家里有法国红酒,所以虽然菜不多,可是颜色十分好看,红是红,白是白,绿是绿,黄是黄。

看到这些,几个人都说,欢欢不再是大家眼里的"小小姐"了,而是一位"超女"!

常苹说:"这些饭菜,还有碗筷盘子的明净,加上这些颜色,让我想起我们中间的一个人。"

谢小星说:"我知道你的意思,是不是……"

## 46

　　常苹突然觉得自己的话头可能不大得体，就想打住，不过这时顾简已经接过话来了，"我明白，常老师说的是我，对吗？"

　　虽然顾简说对了，可是常苹还是觉得很不好意思，就一口气连着说了好几个"对不起"，"对不起，对不起！我这个话说得有一点儿过火了。"

　　"没关系，我不在乎，我的同学和朋友们也常常开这样的玩笑，我已经习惯了。中国有句习语，叫'习惯成自然'，对不对？"

　　常苹接过话头说："对啊！简，我真的觉得你很了不起，把汉语说得那么地道！我来英国以前，已经学了差不多十年的英语，在中国还教英语，现在我到伦敦也有两年多了，可是我的英语常常还是'京歌力师'！"

　　大家听到"京歌力师"都笑得不行。

## 47

　　终于，白书欢在一次发手机短信的时候，同意了钟天明的请求，跟他一道回北京。

　　北京的八月和七月差不多，从早到晚都很热。欢欢除了在自己家里以外，常常去帮助钟天明准备开书店的事。钟天明有了这样一个可爱的小朋友在身边，自然是一天到晚都非常开心。不过，他有一件心事，每当想起来，都不舒服。这件事就是，欢欢很愿意跟他在一起，而且干起工作来，一点儿都不怕累。但是，每次钟天明的爸爸妈妈来的时候，她不但不怎么说话，而且还常常找借口跑到别的地方去，一直到钟天明的爸爸妈妈离开了书店才回来。钟天明虽然感到有些奇怪，可是他不想、也觉得不应该问，因为他知道，他和欢欢的关系还没有到可以告诉家里人的那一步。这层道理他懂，但在感情上，他还是有点儿过不去。

## 48

　　一个雨天，钟天明在没有得到欢欢的同意下，想给她一个意外：主动开车去她的家接她。到了门口，他才发了一条信息。果然，五分钟以后，欢欢出来了。但是没有他想象的那么高兴。钟天明突然脑子一热，想进去看看欢欢的家，也向她的爸爸妈妈问一声好。所以在欢欢从家里出来要上车的时候，他问："欢欢，我可以进去跟你的爸爸妈妈问一个好吗？"

没想到的是，欢欢非但一下子冷下了脸，而且用比她的表情更冰冷的语气回答说："钟天明同学！"这是欢欢与钟天明认识以来头一回这样叫他，"第一，你没经过我的同意就来我家，这本来就已经不太好了；第二，现在你又提出要进到我的家去看看，借口说想问候我的爸爸妈妈，你是不是太过分了。天明，我看还是不必了吧，你还是回去吧。"

## 49

"为什么？我们是好朋友，而且我们都在英国留学，我只是想去看看他们，没有别的意思，来看看好朋友的爸爸妈妈，怎么就不行呢？"钟天明有点儿不高兴了，他觉得欢欢是在故意为难他。

万没有料到的是，欢欢一听这话就更生气了，她二话没说就跑回了家，还把门重重地关上了。

雨越下越大，钟天明的脑子变成了空白，他发现自己都不会思考了。其后，他就像那个自己刻出的马头一样，一动不动、没有知觉。很长时间以后，他才意识到外面的雨声已经没有了，而在光光的街上，他的汽车发动机一直都在响着……

## 50

以后的日子对钟天明来说就不同了：自那天起，白书欢就没有再去过书店。钟天明也没有再给她打电话或者发短信。思来想去，他觉得一定是欢欢的家里发生过什么事情。可是会是什么事情呢？他不知道。慢慢的，这件事就变成了他心里一个解不开的结，结果是他饭也吃不香，觉也睡不好。很快，他的妈妈先发现了这个问题，不过她明白，儿子的事她是问不出来的。于是她把自己的感觉告诉了丈夫。一天，那是在新书店要开始迎接顾客的前一个星期，钟天明突然对他爸爸说："欢欢不会来我们书店帮忙了。"

## 51

"是吗？她回英国了吗？"

"没有，只是她不会再来了。"

"出什么问题了？看样子，她不来对你影响不小，你妈妈早就发现你最近的心情很不正常了。告诉我，你们发生了什么事？"钟天明的爸爸问。

"我也不清楚。"于是，钟天明把那天去接欢欢的前前后后一五一十地说给了爸爸，他希望爸爸能帮助他想想，是不是欢欢的家里有过什么事。

"这个不难，要是你需要，我可以去打听一下。不过，真的有必要吗？天明，欢欢跟你目前是什么关系？"

"这……这很难说。"

"你不说我们也看得出来，最少你对她是有感情的。其实欢欢来了没两天，我们就看出来了。你妈妈在第一次见到她的时候，就附在我的耳朵上说'这个女孩子不简单'。"钟天明的爸爸说。

## 52

"对，你们说得的。我很喜欢她，而且想跟她走得更近，希望她以后能成为我的女朋友。但是，她近些天的所作所为，实在让我很担心。要是她这么不懂事，不顾别人的感觉，今后我们怎么在一起呢？"

"天明，先不要急着怪她，你也应该做一做调查。我认为很有可能是她的家有过什么事，所以她不想要你进她的家，更不想让你见她的亲人。对了，你妈妈还说过，我们每次去书店的时候，她的样子都不很自然，而且十次有九次都借故跑开，不和我们在一起。"

"这个我早就知道，可是跟你们一样，我也不清楚是为什么。"钟天明说。"虽然我们在英国来往得很多，差不多一两个星期就见一次面，平时也发发短信，可是我从来没有问过她家里是做什么的。我只知道她住的地方是个高干楼，因为楼已经很旧了，我想里边住的那些人可能都是过去的高干，不是现在的。楼已经很旧了。其他的我就都不了解了。您怎么调查呢？我也上网试过，可是因为我不知道她爸爸的名字和单位，所以什么都没有查到。"

"这样吧，我们都留意一些，我也帮助你问问。"

……

# 附录 Appendix

## Character List
## 本册汉字索引表

| Character codes | Character | Pinyin | English |
|---|---|---|---|
| 349 | 阿 | ā; ē | Prefix |
| 350 | 啊 | ā; á; ǎ; à | WOW |
| 351 | 矮 | ǎi | SHORT |
| 352 | 安 | ān | PEACE/SAFETY |
| 353 | 把 | bǎ | HOLD |
| 354 | 般 | bān | TYPE/LIKE |
| 355 | 搬 | bān | MOVE |
| 356 | 板 | bǎn | BOARD |
| 357 | 办（辦） | bàn | DEAL/DO/MANAGE |
| 358 | 半 | bàn | HALF |
| 359 | 包 | bāo | WRAP |
| 360 | 饱（飽） | bǎo | FULL |
| 361 | 被 | bèi | QUILT |
| 362 | 鼻 | bí | NOSE |
| 363 | 必 | bì | MUST |
| 364 | 变（變） | biàn | CHANGE |
| 365 | 冰 | bīng | ICE |
| 366 | 才 | cái | JUST |
| 367 | 参（參） | cān | PARTICIPATE |
| 368 | 草 | cǎo | GRASS |
| 369 | 层（層） | céng | STOREY/LAYER |
| 370 | 查 | chá | CHECK |
| 371 | 差 | chà | BAD |
| 371 | 差 | chā | DIFFERENCE |
| 372 | 尝（嘗） | cháng | TASTE |
| 373 | 超 | chāo | SURPASS |
| 374 | 衬 | chèn | INNER LINING |
| 375 | 成 | chéng | BECOME |
| 376 | 城 | chéng | CITY/WALL |
| 377 | 迟（遲） | chí | LATE |
| 378 | 除 | chú | EXCEPT |
| 379 | 楚 | chǔ | CLEAR |
| 380 | 船 | chuán | BOAT |
| 381 | 春 | chūn | SPRING |
| 382 | 词（詞） | cí | WORD |
| 383 | 聪（聰） | cōng | CLEVER |
| 384 | 答 | dā | AGREE |
| 384 | 答 | dá | ANSWER |
| 385 | 带（帶） | dài | BELT |
| 386 | 单（單） | dān | SINGLE |
| 387 | 担（擔） | dān | WORRY |
| 387 | 担（擔） | dàn | BURDEN |

（续表）

| Character codes | Character | Pinyin | English |
|---|---|---|---|
| 388 | 当（當） | dāng | WHEN/BE |
|  |  | dàng | PROPER |
| 389 | 灯（燈） | dēng | LAMP/LIGHT |
| 390 | 地 | dì | LAND/SOIL |
|  |  | de | Grammatical Code |
| 391 | 典 | diǎn | CLASSIC |
| 392 | 定 | dìng | STABILITY |
| 393 | 冬 | dōng | WINTER |
| 394 | 短 | duǎn | SHORT |
| 395 | 段 | duàn | SECTION |
| 396 | 锻（鍛） | duàn | FORGE |
| 397 | 朵 | duǒ | Measure Word |
| 398 | 饿（餓） | è | HUNGRY |
| 399 | 而 | ér | BUT |
| 400 | 耳 | ěr | EAR |
| 401 | 发（發/髮） | fā | LAUNCH |
|  |  | fà | HAIR |
| 402 | 法 | fǎ | METHOD/LAW |
|  |  | fá | METHOD |
| 403 | 方 | fāng | SQUARE |
| 404 | 放 | fàng | PUT |
| 405 | 风（風） | fēng | WIND |
| 406 | 附 | fù | AFFILIATE/ATTACH |
| 407 | 复（復/複） | fù | REPEAT |
| 408 | 该（該） | gāi | OUGHT TO/SHOULD |
| 409 | 干（幹/乾） | gān | DRY |
|  |  | gàn | DO |
| 410 | 感 | gǎn | FEELING |
| 411 | 刚（剛） | gāng | JUST |
| 412 | 糕 | gāo | CAKE |
| 413 | 根 | gēn | ROOT |
| 414 | 跟 | gēn | HEEL/WITH/FOLLOW |
| 415 | 更 | gēng | CHANGE |
|  |  | gèng | MORE |
| 416 | 故 | gù | OLD |
| 417 | 顾（顧） | gù | LOOK |
| 418 | 刮 | guā | BLOW |
| 419 | 怪 | guài | STRANGE |
| 420 | 惯（慣） | guàn | HABIT |
| 421 | 害 | hài | HARM |
| 422 | 行 | háng | BUSINESS |
|  |  | xíng | WALK |
| 423 | 河 | hé | RIVER |
| 424 | 乎 | hū | Particle |
| 425 | 护（護） | hù | PROTECT |
| 426 | 花 | huā | FLOWER |
| 427 | 化 | huà | CHANGE |
| 428 | 画（畫） | huà | PAINTING/DRAWING |
| 429 | 坏 | huài | BAD |
| 430 | 环（環） | huán | CIRCLE |
| 431 | 换 | huàn | REPLACE |

(续表)

| Character codes | Character | Pinyin | English |
|---|---|---|---|
| 432 | 黄 | huáng | YELLOW |
| 433 | 婚 | hūn | MARRIAGE |
| 434 | 或 | huò | OR |
| 435 | 级（級） | jí | GRADE/LEVEL |
| 436 | 极（極） | jí | EXTREME |
| 437 | 急 | jí | HURRY/ANXIOUS |
| 438 | 己 | jǐ | SELF |
| 439 | 记（記） | jì | TAKE NOTE |
| 440 | 季 | jì | SEASON |
| 441 | 绩（績） | jì | ACHIEVEMENT |
| 442 | 加 | jiā | ADD |
| 443 | 假 | jiǎ | FALSE |
| 443 | 假 | jià | HOLIDAY |
| 444 | 检（檢） | jiǎn | CHECK |
| 445 | 简（簡） | jiǎn | SIMPLE |
| 446 | 健 | jiàn | SOUND/HEALTHY |
| 447 | 讲（講） | jiǎng | SPEECH |
| 448 | 蕉 | jiāo | BANANA |
| 449 | 角 | jiǎo | HORN/CORNER |
| 449 | 角 | jué | ROLE |
| 450 | 脚 | jiǎo | FOOT |
| 451 | 较（較） | jiào | COMPARISON |
| 452 | 接 | jiē | BRING IN/RECEIVE |
| 453 | 街 | jiē | STREET |
| 454 | 节（節） | jié | FESTIVAL |
| 455 | 结（結） | jié | JOIN |
| 455 | 结（結） | jiē | PRODUCE |
| 456 | 解 | jiě | DISSECT |
| 457 | 界 | jiè | BOUNDARY |
| 458 | 借 | jiè | BORROW |
| 459 | 斤 | jīn | 500 GRAMS |
| 460 | 净 | jìng | CLEAN |
| 461 | 静 | jìng | QUIET |
| 462 | 境 | jìng | BORDER |
| 463 | 久 | jiǔ | LONG |
| 464 | 酒 | jiǔ | ALCOHOL |
| 465 | 旧（舊） | jiù | OLD |
| 466 | 居 | jū | LIVE |
| 467 | 句 | jù | SENTENCE |
| 468 | 据 | jù | ACCORDING |
| 469 | 决 | jué | DECIDE |
| 470 | 卡 | kǎ | CARD |
| 470 | 卡 | qiǎ | CLIP |
| 471 | 康 | kāng | HEALTH |
| 472 | 渴 | kě | THIRSTY |
| 473 | 刻 | kè | ENGRAVE |
| 474 | 空 | kōng | EMPTY |
| 474 | 空 | kòng | BLANK |
| 475 | 口 | kǒu | MOUTH |
| 476 | 哭 | kū | CRY |
| 477 | 裤（褲） | kù | TROUSERS |

（续表）

| Character codes | Character | Pinyin | English |
|---|---|---|---|
| 478 | 筷 | kuài | CHOPSTICKS |
| 479 | 蓝（藍） | lán | BLUE |
| 480 | 礼（禮） | lǐ | CEREMONY |
| 481 | 李 | lǐ | PLUM |
| 482 | 理 | lǐ | REASON |
| 483 | 力 | lì | FORCE/POWER |
| 484 | 历 | lì | EXPERIENCE |
| 485 | 脸（臉） | liǎn | FACE |
| 486 | 练（練） | liàn | PRACTICE |
| 487 | 炼（煉） | liàn | REFINE |
| 488 | 辆（輛） | liàng | MW for VEHICLES |
| 489 | 聊 | liáo | CHAT |
| 490 | 料 | liào | STUFF |
| 491 | 邻（鄰） | lín | NEIGHBOUR |
| 492 | 留 | liú | STAY |
| 493 | 楼（樓） | lóu | STORIED BUILDING |
| 494 | 绿（綠） | lǜ | GREEN |
| 495 | 马（馬） | mǎ | HORSE |
| 496 | 满 | mǎn | SATISFIED |
| 497 | 冒 | mào | EVAPORATE |
| 498 | 帽 | mào | CAP |
| 499 | 末 | mò | END |
| 500 | 目 | mù | EYE |
| 501 | 拿 | ná | PICK UP |
| 502 | 南 | nán | SOUTH |
| 503 | 难（難） | nán | DIFFICULT |
| | | nàn | DISASTER |
| 504 | 鸟（鳥） | niǎo | BIRD |
| 505 | 努 | nǔ | HARD WORK |
| 506 | 爬 | pá | CLIMB |
| 507 | 怕 | pà | AFRAID/FEAR |
| 508 | 盘（盤） | pán | PLATE |
| 509 | 胖 | pàng | FAT |
| 510 | 皮 | pí | SKIN |
| 511 | 啤 | pí | BEER |
| 512 | 片 | piàn | PIECE |
| | | piān (-r) | Orally Rhotic |
| 513 | 平 | píng | FLAT/LEVEL |
| 514 | 瓶 | píng | BOTTLE |
| 515 | 其 | qí | IT/THAT |
| 516 | 奇 | qí | STRANGE |
| 517 | 骑（騎） | qí | RIDE |
| 518 | 且 | qiě | ADD/EVEN MORE |
| 519 | 轻（輕） | qīng | LIGHT |
| 520 | 清 | qīng | CLEAR |
| 521 | 秋 | qiū | AUTUMN |
| 522 | 求 | qiú | ASK FOR |
| 523 | 趣 | qù | FUN/INTERESTING |
| 524 | 裙 | qún | SKIRT |
| 525 | 容 | róng | ACCOMMODATE |
| 526 | 如 | rú | SIMILAR |

（续表）

| Character codes | Character | Pinyin | English |
|---|---|---|---|
| 527 | 赛（賽） | sài | MATCH |
| 528 | 伞（傘） | sǎn | UMBRELLA |
| 529 | 扫（掃） | sào | BROOM |
|  |  | sǎo | SWEEP |
| 530 | 山 | shān | MOUNTAIN |
| 531 | 衫 | shān | SHIRT |
| 532 | 烧（燒） | shāo | BURN |
| 533 | 声（聲） | shēng | SOUND |
| 534 | 实（實） | shí | PRACTICAL |
| 535 | 史 | shǐ | HISTORY |
| 536 | 世（丗） | shì | CENTURY |
| 537 | 市 | shì | MARKET |
| 538 | 瘦 | shòu | THIN |
| 539 | 叔 | shū | UNCLE |
| 540 | 舒 | shū | COMFORTABLE |
| 541 | 束 | shù | BUNCH |
| 542 | 树 | shù | TREE |
| 543 | 数（數） | shù | NUMBER |
|  |  | shǔ | TO COUNT |
| 544 | 刷 | shuā | SCRUB |
| 545 | 双（雙） | shuāng | A PAIR |
| 546 | 算 | suàn | CALCULATE |
| 547 | 特 | tè | SPECIAL |
| 548 | 疼 | téng | PAIN |
| 549 | 梯 | tī | LADDER/STAIRS |
| 550 | 提 | tí | CARRY/LIFT |
| 551 | 甜 | tián | SWEET |
| 552 | 调（調） | tiáo | ADJUST |
|  |  | diào | ALLOCATE |
| 553 | 铁（鐵） | tiě | IRON |
| 554 | 头（頭） | tóu | HEAD |
| 555 | 突 | tū | SUDDEN |
| 556 | 图（圖） | tú | PICTURE |
| 557 | 腿 | tuǐ | LEG |
| 558 | 碗 | wǎn | BOWL |
| 559 | 万（萬） | wàn | TEN THOUSAND |
| 560 | 网（網） | wǎng | NET |
| 561 | 忘 | wàng | FORGET |
| 562 | 位 | wèi | POSITION |
| 563 | 文 | wén | CHARACTER |
| 564 | 闻（聞） | wén | HEAR |
| 565 | 物 | wù | MATTER/THING |
| 566 | 戏（戲） | xì | DRAMA |
| 567 | 夏 | xià | SUMMER |
| 568 | 鲜（鮮） | xiān | FRESH |
| 569 | 相 | xiāng | SEE/EACH OTHER |
|  |  | xiàng | PICTURE |
| 570 | 香 | xiāng | DELICIOUS |
| 571 | 箱 | xiāng | BOX/CASE |
| 572 | 响（響） | xiǎng | SOUND |
| 573 | 向 | xiàng | TOWARDS |

（续表）

| Character codes | Character | Pinyin | English |
|---|---|---|---|
| 574 | 像 | xiàng | IMAGE |
| 575 | 鞋 | xié | SHOE |
| 576 | 心 | xīn | HEART |
| 577 | 信 | xìn | TRUST |
| 578 | 熊 | xióng | BEAR |
| 579 | 须 | xū | BEARD |
| 580 | 需 | xū | NEED |
| 581 | 选（選） | xuǎn | SELECT |
| 582 | 牙 | yá | TEETH |
| 583 | 阳（陽） | yáng | SUN |
| 584 | 爷 | yé | GRANDFATHER |
| 585 | 业（業） | yè | LINE OF BUSINESS |
| 586 | 姨 | yí | AUNT |
| 587 | 议（議） | yì | DISCUSS |
| 588 | 易 | yì | CHANGE |
| 589 | 音 | yīn | MUSIC |
| 590 | 银（銀） | yín | SILVER |
| 591 | 饮（飲） | yǐn | DRINK |
| 592 | 应（應） | yīng | SHOULD |
| | | yìng | RESPOND |
| 593 | 迎 | yíng | WELCOME |
| 594 | 用 | yòng | USE |
| 595 | 邮 | yóu | POST |
| 596 | 又 | yòu | AGAIN |
| 597 | 于 | yú | AT |
| 598 | 育 | yù | RAISE |
| 599 | 遇 | yù | MEET |
| 600 | 元 | yuán | ORIGIN |
| 601 | 园（園） | yuán | GARDEN/PARK |
| 602 | 愿 | yuàn | WISH |
| 603 | 越 | yuè | SURPASS |
| 604 | 澡 | zǎo | BATH |
| 605 | 择（擇） | zé | CHOOSE |
| 606 | 张（張） | zhāng | BE OPENED |
| 607 | 照 | zhào | ILLUMINATE |
| 608 | 者 | zhě | PERSON |
| 609 | 直 | zhí | STRAIGHT |
| 610 | 终（終） | zhōng | BE OVER |
| 611 | 种（種） | zhǒng | SEED |
| | | zhòng | PLANT |
| 612 | 重 | zhòng | HEAVY |
| | | chóng | REPEAT |
| 613 | 周 | zhōu | SURROUNDING |
| 614 | 主 | zhǔ | MAIN/MASTER |
| 615 | 注 | zhù | ATTENTION |
| 616 | 自 | zì | ONESELF |
| 617 | 总（總） | zǒng | SUM UP |
| 618 | 嘴 | zuǐ | MOUTH |

出版策划：王君校　　韩　晖
统筹协调：付　眉　韩　颖　彭　博
策划编辑：陆　瑜
责任编辑：陆　瑜
英文编辑：韩芙芸

**图书在版编目（CIP）数据**

118小时突破中级中文．练习册．上册：汉英 / 苏立群主编．-- 北京：华语教学出版社，2021.4
ISBN 978-7-5138-2066-0

Ⅰ．①1… Ⅱ．①苏… Ⅲ．①汉语－对外汉语教学－教材 Ⅳ．① H195.4

中国版本图书馆CIP数据核字（2020）第264879号

**118小时突破中级中文．练习册（上册）**

LIQUN SU（苏立群） 主编

\*

©华语教学出版社有限责任公司
华语教学出版社有限责任公司出版
（中国北京百万庄大街24号　邮政编码 100037）
电话：(86)10-68320585　68997826
传真：(86)10-68997826　68326333
网址：www.sinolingua.com.cn
电子信箱：hyjx@sinolingua.com.cn
北京虎彩文化传播有限公司印刷
2021年（16开）第1版
2021年第1版第1次印刷
ISBN 978-7-5138-2066-0
005500